grief
Climb
Toward
Understanding

grief
Climb
Toward
Understanding

Self-help when
you are struggling

*Includes checklists
of what you can do*

By Phyllis Davies

Illustrations by Itoko Maeno

Sunnybank Publishers
San Luis Obispo, California

Published by

Sunnybank Publishers
P.O. Box 945
San Luis Obispo, California 93406

Queries regarding rights and permissions
should be addressed to: Sunnybank Publishers,
P.O. Box 945, San Luis Obispo, CA 93406.

Library of Congress Cataloging in Publication Data:

Davies, Phyllis, 1941-
    Grief: climb toward understanding: self-help when you are
struggling: includes checklists of what you can do/by Phyllis
Davies: Illustrations by Itoko Maeno — 4th ed.
    p. cm.
    Includes index.
    ISBN 0-941343-30-8 (pbk.)
    1. Bereavement — Psychological aspects. 2. Grief.
    3. Teenagers — Death — Psychological aspects.
    4. Loss (Psychology)
    I. Title.
BF575.G7D39
155.9'37–dc20   96-3611
                                         CIP

Design consultant: Margaret Dodd
Manufactured in the United States of America

ISBN 0-941343-39-1 (pbk.)

First Edition   1987
Second Edition   1988
Third Edition   1993
Fourth Edition   1996
Fifth Edition   1998

Canadian and United Kingdom content.   Cover and book printed on ♻ paper

To Bill and Dawna

Contents

3rd NEW ORDER 93

Preface

On a clear, cloudless, late summer morning our thirteen-year-old son, Derek, and I drove to the airport. He was going on a vacation to his uncle's ranch after a summer of hard work on our farm. Out of sight, four minutes after we waved and as the commercial airliner took off, it collided mid-air with a small plane. No one survived. Derek was dead.

Within a few weeks, I was a volcano ready to explode. I was caught in a blurring steam with a magma of memories swirling around me. I could no longer think clearly. Memories of Derek completely occupied my mind. Our two children laughing and playing together. Our large extended family working together on farm projects, gardening and canning. The four of us going to dances and traveling as a family. Enjoying our music, his roping and football. Love for family and others – even pets, places, objects, and life itself – was equaled by the depth of our sorrow.

It was in sorrow as I groped in pain through the memories of what life had been and my dreams of the future, that I began to write in a notebook. As I did, I began to see and feel my pain, my life, my growth. These thoughts flowed into this free verse story.

Grief felt like I was lost and crawling around on and across mountains on my hands and knees. I eventually began to discover that this agony was part of my own growth process. My writings naturally fell into five categories. I metaphorically interpret them as five summits where I climbed, crawled, slipped back, got lost and finally stood to walk across and "refocus" on a new part of my life. All of a sudden, again, my focus shifted, as if I was seeing through the clear lens of a camera.

You will come to know my husband Bill and our teenage daughter Dawna through my writings, and as you read the transcription of Derek's Memorial Service in *Our Good-bye*, beginning on *page* 178. We have had contrasting grief experiences. We found we knew Derek from different perspectives, although we had all been close to him. We each had a unique partnership with him, as well as being players on our family team. Struggling through this grief – both together and alone – has increased my love and admiration for Bill and Dawna. These have been exceedingly difficult years.

When Dawna was a year old, we had a son who died as he was born. I closed off those awful memories. I couldn't cope with them and didn't know how to ask for help or even that help was available. In the middle of my grief for Derek, I suddenly discovered an immense amount of unfinished grief for our baby. Seventeen years after his death, we named him Dylan. Today his simple grave marker is next to Derek's in the grove of trees between our house and barn overlooking the valley.

Grief is as individual as a snowflake and is the adjustment to change. Yet, there is a healing process that usually becomes evident in the intense emotional stress around loss, disaster and life change. Death creates grief. It is not the only kind of grief, although it is often the most disorienting and devastating.

Living on a diversified farm with animals, our family has experienced grief as an integral part of life. Especially when a pet dies or even when a farm animal is sold or dies, I have dealt with degrees of grief. I experience grief when a friend moves, copes with serious illness or injury and loss of good health or when a divorce between friends occurs. I have felt grief's presence even in life's happy moments, such as graduations, retirement, promotions and weddings, because these all require changes.

I have no illusions of literary excellence. This was not written to be a book. It was merely my survival notebook. I wrote these lyric prose pieces for myself. They helped my healing process, and later others discovered help or encouragement from them in their struggle across their own mountains of loss.

You'll find included with my writing two meaningful poems written by others.

The checklists and other information in the extensive reference section are my response to coping pro-actively with decisions that we as a family have found are important to consider when a death occurs. They stand in harsh contrast to the free verse. Yet, I feel they warrant inclusion as they are a profound part of my story.

Grief comes with life. Seeing and feeling this map of the general terrain of the five overlapping and interlaced phases or mountains helped me to work through my grief process. With time, I've found new purpose and joy in life.

In a time of grief, I hope this collection will serve as a map and inspire you to begin to unlock your own hurt, anger, sorrow and joy on paper – throughout your journey.

Phyllis Davies

Note: The day this book went to press, we received this precious note from Derek's classmates, years after his death. I want to share it with you. *"We want you to know we remember Derek. He walked so lightly and responsibly on this earth all the years we went to school with him. The power of his gentle thoughtfulness and competence continues to walk beside us. We have listed him 'In Memory' as a member of our class at San Luis Obispo High School."*

Writing as a Tool for Healing

After Derek's death I needed to write down my memories, yet I was afraid. All my life, attempts to write have been hampered by learning disabilities that make writing and reading difficult. Something naggingly encouraged me to enroll in a writing workshop and try one more time.

My grief experiences and memories unfolded onto paper through the ideas and exercises introduced in the suggested text, Writing the Natural Way, by Gabriele Rico. It helped me cut the chains of failure and criticism that had bound me since childhood.

The release from grief has been slow – two steps ahead, one or even three back. At times the paper was so wet with tears it would tear as I wrote the next word, so I would start again on another sheet of paper. Writing about thoughts, experiences, feelings and flashbacks as they occurred helped me heal.

The "clustering" process from Gabriele's book has been particularly helpful to me and for others in writing groups. We continue to return to the tools in her book to re-inspire our writing.

Most of the pieces, in their original form, have been written to Derek or to both him and Dylan. Upon finishing each writing, I have felt relief and pleasure, accompanied by another level of closeness to each son. It feels much like sitting and talking, sharing thoughts with them or a very dear friend.

Writing has helped me enter fully into my sorrow. In doing so, I began to discover that there are gifts hidden in the grief experience. Although there has been great sorrow from our sons' deaths, there has been great joy in sharing and helping others with their own sorrow. This has helped me progress through grief to a release and peace. Most of the time, I now can remember Derek and Dylan without crying inside or out.

Writing is a creative expression that has helped me keep my commitment to grow through the experiences I face and to live in the present rather than the past.

Climb Toward Understanding

628 *or* 624

No one
would tell
us anything.

Radio report.

A midair collision.
Wings West Flight 628.

11:17 a.m.

"Wings West 624 – 11:00"
was written in
my daily log.

All
phones
busy –
airlines,
airport.

We went to the
airport in person.
"I'm sorry; we have no information."

No information!!

It's *your* plane crash!

Hospital
emergency room.
"No survivors from 628."

"But was there a 624 at 11:00?"

A flash of anger.

RED-HOT STEEL

branded

Hours passed.
Not knowing,
we waited,

life
forever

prayed,
waited,
waited.

BEFORE   624

3:00.
Derek's
arrival time,
Reno Airport.

and

AFTER   628.

Phoned.
        No answer.
Again,
        busy signals.
Again,
        busy.

Again,
        finally
                someone answered.

We asked,
"Would you
   please page
      Derek Davies?"

We waited

      waited

         waited.

Coldly: "No answer to the page."

So we waited,
            waited.

After dark
the sheriff called.

"Your son's body
   has been identified."

There had been no 624.

Only 628.

Derek is dead.

Derek is dead?
Waiting.
Waited.

What?

D E R E K

D E A D

Wait, what?
Derek, dead.

Derek . . .

         No waiting.

      Wait . . .

I want to wait a minute more.

Five-Summit Journey

Suddenly
trapped and tied
in aimless struggle.
Lashed by emotion,
unknown gales.

Slowly, I began to see
what was happening,
to understand grief
is a crawling,
        slipping,
            falling,
                climbing process.

Mountains,
layered millennia
loomed ahead above me –
a range of strange-named peaks.

SHOCK,
the first summit
caught me unprepared
for the grueling
crawling climb
on my hands
my knees.

On the peak of
DISORDERED SUFFERING
the storms of memories
lashed me constantly.

NEW ORDER,
a third
more scalable crag,
evolved before my eyes
out of that blizzard.

PERSPECTIVE,
summit four,
revealed fresh concepts
neither seen nor felt before,
cautiously emerging from the fog.

REFOCUS,
a small knoll,
demands a courageous walk,
as the sun sets into grieving twilight.

The first
three summits
inner-driven
exhausting climbs.

Peak three,
NEW ORDER,
is where life
begins to be
almost tolerable again,

I stop, rest, and ask,

    "Why go on?"

Yet
I must
trudge on!
That little "can do it"
"you can, can do it"
a whisper, gets louder.
"Keep on, climb on"
you can make it over
this mountain.

How many die still crying?

Bewildered,
I looked out across
the last two summits:
PERSPECTIVE
then
REFOCUS.

Healing came
by crossing
all summits
and their valleys.

Unresolved
grief,
a leach,
sucks out
all one has
to give to life.

Its cost is
beyond belief
for you, for me,
for lives we touch
and for our world.

Structure and support
imbeds in webs
of custom,
"luto,"
"shiva,"
"the wake,"
"widow's weeds,"
the "mourning year,"
once guided us.

Time-honored
traditions
now lost,
as our culture
became a mix of many,
no longer urge us on.
Celebrations were our
milestone markers,
cheers along
grief's way.

Bereavement
differs greatly.
Now
I understand
grief as a process.

I urge you,
even if it's been
fifty years of grieving,
get up, go on across
that final hill **REFOCUS.**

Join me in saying
"Thank you, Grief."

I am who
I am today,
in part,
because
I have crossed
five summits.

This Book

I'm looking back across
these peaks of grief,
I see those paths
I crawled.

Trails worn through rock,
washed with tears
since time began.

For me,
it's been
a journey
of two years.

My hand drew this map.
It's here for you to use.

As I set it down,
just know
I'll walk
this trail again
with you, if you wish.

It's easier for me now
to cross this mountain range.
I know the trail – felt the process.
I've seen the panoramic peace.

As we walk,
we'll marvel
at what once
went unnoticed.

You'll meet,
grow to know
two of my gentle,
loving teachers, our sons.

Shock

Unexpected.
Mountain.
Cruel cliffs.

No pitons.
No crampons,
just
bare feet
and crawling.

Water freezes.
Ice expands.
Pressure builds.
Boulders split.
Glaciers melt.
Shale showers.

Numb.

Angry.
Fearful.
Relieved.
Panicked.
Sleepless.

Irrational.
Anesthetized.
Perceptive.
Courageous,
then a stoic hazy-blur
or
possibly even
the peace-filled clarity
of my time on this peak.

This can't be real.

Disbelief grabs,
time suspends
in this cold dark
summit's spell.

Recognition

Even though
we didn't know,
wouldn't know...
for hours.

We stood
in our office.
Bill held me,
we prayed:

"Dear Lord,
    give us strength
        to help those who need us."

"Let us remember we are growing
    through the experience ahead.
        Please hold Derek — all of us
            in Your Light and Love."

We drove home to be with Dawna.

She needed to know.

We needed
to be together.

Derek
was likely
on one of the planes
that had collided.

We waited.

The three of us waited.

Waiting.
I kept
refocusing
my awareness
on God's Light and Love
around each person,
on those flights, on through
the first hours of their transition.

Angels and Ashes

Angel clouds
dancing,
coconut sorbet swirls
floated onto that cloudless
dusking sky.

Angels
welcoming
the departed travelers
celebrating
in that lemon
      apricot
        raspberry
           boysenberry sunset.

I saw a vision

of the instant after
the collision.

His death.

Rising
from
twisted
burning
wreckage,
he turned,
extending his hand
to the others,
saying,
"Come on,
   don't hold back.
     We all have jobs to do."

They
flew on,
leaving
the old clothes
their bodies
behind in the ashes.

Untitled

Unknown to me
seventeen die in midair collision.

that evening i see clouds looking
like an ensemble of dancing angels.

miles southward native people say
is where souls depart this land.

preachers of faith and ministers of science
blow tremendous winds about such puzzles
never arriving at the truth.

the clouds extend their arms and move onward.

KARL KEMPTON

Note: *Months after I wrote ANGELS AND ASHES, the poet Karl Kempton, whom we had not known, asked, "Would you like a copy of the poem I wrote the day your son, Derek died?" Above you will find his untitled poem.*
We have no photos taken of the angles described in ANGELS AND ASHES and UNTITLED. When you check the Internet, http:/flight 800.sunlink.net/picture.html for "Angel Among Us" photo, you will find a similar single angel taken after the TWA flight 800 tragedy.

Our Child Is Dead

Those parts of Bill,
those parts of me,
a thousand facets
uniquely shone
in our child.

Loved.
Nurtured.
Vanished.

We thought
we had given
the world this son
to carry on:
lessons,
values,
love.

He vanished
in *one* moment.

Gone.

Gone

On the slope
of one of the hills
encircling us,
he left this life
of thirteen years
in an instant.

The plane
collided midair
with another
on its climb
into that
aqua silk
sky.

Moments before
at the boarding gate
he gave me one of those
almost grown-up
almost embarrassed
"I-want-to,
  but-
    not-here-Mom" hugs.

Waving
he turned,
his smile
filled the space
between us.

My last words
still echo off our hills
"Have a wonderful time, Derek.
  We love you."

        You

           you

            you

              bounce

          back to me

     endlessly.

Why <u>That</u> Night ?

My lifelong pattern
of sleeping well

broke

a year
before
you died.

Increasing
restlessness.

Strange shifts
started slowly,
imperceptibly.

Checking
children
as I came
down the hall.

Derek
first,
nearest
the door,
then
Dawna.

A gentle touch,
then a whisper,
"We love you."

They must
have heard me,
a smile
would cross each face.

Living room,
stoke the fire,
read or work
awhile.

Productive
project hours
mixed with
looking in on
children
several
times.

I never
asked myself
"Why do I feel
   this growing need
      to touch them?"

No fear,
it just felt
warmly *"motherly"*
to see, to know
they were sleeping
peacefully.

Less,

less sleep
and
less sleep.

Yet
I would
awaken, rested,
as their 4:30 alarm
started a new day with chores.

Strangely

that night,

the night
of the day
you died,
tranquil,
uninterrupted
sleep

returned.

Mourning After

I awake,
aware of
mourning
the morning
after you die.

Yet I am
in a river of light,
floating unobstructed
in high, fast energy.

Suddenly
synchronized
in rapid flow
with those around me,
even unmet, unknown,

Intuition floodgates open...

Memorial service
arrangements
details
flow
together
effortlessly,
as do my words
as I stand to speak
to those hundreds
who come to celebrate you.

Then, days move to weeks,

A parking space
or someone pulling out,
always where I need to park,

Impossible
in our town.
Yet that's how it is.

Phone rings
as I reach to dial.
It's the person
I'm calling!

People
I need to see
I meet by *accident*?

Verse
suddenly
begins to flow
from my heart
through unused pen.

Transparency
keeps me from
timidly holding
what I wouldn't have had
the courage to share before.

Leaving
my body
part of me
watches my pain,
until
healing peace returns.

Answers
come before
questions are asked.

Decisions,
accurate leaps,
all facts considered
seemingly without aim.

Vision.
  I *see*.
  I know
she's
  pregnant,
    a daughter.

She cuddles
  her,

    exactly

nine months later.

Intuition:
  poignant
    crystals,
vivid,
  trusted,
    accurate.

Now
  each
    moment,
  all important,
  each person,
  precious,
  unique.

I'm
strangely
unaware of time.

Those first six months
a mystic consistency
almost frightening.

When briefly
  clouded
    in storm,
     tears come,
then clear to rainbows.

Connectedness,
to all place,
all time.

New
yet
now I know
has it always been?

A friend
speaks wisdom.

Bewildered.

"This will change.
  It did for me.
    You must *choose*
      to stay in light."

   Why me?

     Why now?

Reminded of my childhood song.

*This light that I have
  the world didn't give to me.
What the world didn't give
  the world can't take away.*

As months pass,
  that simple melody
    often returns me to
our synchronistic river.

Our Valley

Our hills
  hold us.
    We cry gently.

They whisper
seasonal melodies.

I am a child
  cradled and lulled
    in my mother's arms.

Hills and friends
  still surround,
    softly comfort us.

We deeply
appreciate
all of you,
the prayers,
support, and concern,
from you, our friends,
in this gentle valley.

These encircling hills
  remind me that
    we are truly held
      in His
        everlasting arms.

Holding You

The morning after
your memorial service.

I stopped
at the mortuary
to get your
ashes –
a little box,
"cremains."

I needed
to hold you
after you died.

Wasn't it only yesterday,
I held you in my arms
after you were born
when your father
drove us home.

I needed
to bring you
home once more.

The box
was heavier
than I expected.

I felt
unforgettably
connected to you
as I held it
on my lap.

Was the car
on automatic pilot?
My only memory
of the trip home
is holding
your box.

Through tears,
those cherished memories,
those timeless words
You were home again.   blended into comfort.

Home again
here on the farm
in this valley.

We each
held the box
of your ashes.

Then
we laid
the heavy
little box
gently to rest
here on the farm

in this land you loved.

Later

"Remember,
    your time
        will be
            later,
                alone."

Everyone needed me.

Decisions,
        decisions,
                decisions.

Often their greatest
need
was to help.
Doing something
dissipates anguish,
despair.

I had to learn
to accept,
not to resist,
a need to help.

New resilience
came, as I learned
of death and grief,
responding to others.

"What can I do?"

Friends
visited;
dusted,
cooked,
did dishes,
cut firewood,
aided my healing.

Their healing came.

The hard work of grief
was ahead of me,
alone.

My wise friend was right.
"For you, he'll die many times,
    for a time, each new day.
        Yes, he'll die many, many times.

Your time will be later, alone."
It was later,
    much, much later,

            many, many times later,

And alone.

Bonded

My heart

screams

again
when I hear
of your child
missing or dead.

I am bonded
to you my sisters,
        my brothers.

I intuit
your anguish
across all time,
        all lands.

50,000 missing in Guatemala.
        50,000 people
                disappeared?
                        No answers?

    All our sons and daughters.

Grocery bag pictures.
    Milk carton pictures.
        Famine, torture, war.

Bosnia,
Rwanda,
Vietnam,
Auschwitz,
Nicaragua,
Hiroshima,
Oklahoma City,
Dunblane,
TWA Flight 800,
row upon row,
        gravestones
                march across my life.

At least
I know what
happened to my sons…
Knowing helped me heal.

You, too,
have placed
your child's name
on a missing list,
a grave.

You too
have asked
Why go on?

My soul embraces you.

Notes on my own memories of shock…

Disordered Suffering

This rugged
second mountain,
jumbled jagged rocks
of memories and emotions.

Each boulder, stone, crack
holds an explosive
pain-filled memory.
It hurts to breath.
Sighs – get more air?
As I crawl and climb
I stumble, fall,
slip back.

Recollections
haunt and scramble,
confused and beaten
by relentless winds
amidst these
tortured
crags.

Apathy, antagonism, remorse
bewilderment, panic
blend into
bitter,
blank
depression.
No compass, lost within,
isolation's wilderness.
Each memory, a crystal
in gale-force snowstorms.
Thunderheads of sorrows
boil around this peak
in poignant images.
Impoverished hysteria,
rockslides of guilt
huddle in a heap,
unbalanced.
Wounded,
sobbing.
Angry.

Is It ?

Death isn't fair.

It isn't fair.

It isn't fair,

is it?

In Triplicate
In Triplicate
In Triplicate

Our mail comes
   to an old brown barn mailbox
      with its rusty, red metal flag.

I stop
  get mail,
    turn onto
rutted road
into our valley.

Open —
thick envelope.
Return address —
Health Department.

Of course...
The long-awaited
"Well Water Report."

Why does it take so...
so long to get reports?

I open it.
My eyes fly
to typed words,
look for "acceptable"
quantity and quality.

First word
  stops my eyes,
    sears
      into my memory.

My breath
vanishes
with facts
not known,
vacuumed out,
instant nausea,
vomiting,
days of depression,
reeling out of balance.

The death certificate,
   in triplicate
    in triplicate
      in triplicate...

Relationship

Living
constellates
into one-on-one
attract — repel,
balance of unseen forces.

Families orbit.
Constellations,   Death
relationships.   disrupts
Interlaced.   the balance.
Entangled.
Layered.   Those left
Teamed.   must let go.
One-
  on-   I *must* let go,
    one.

       He is gone.

       Those left
       grieve alone.

       I grieve alone,
       even in a loving family
       of one-on-one
           one-on-one
              one-on-one

       relationships.

Kicked

Death kicked
our family box.

Four sides
now three.

A triangle
is not a
box.

Marriage – Family – Death

Hold on,
keep in touch with each other
when death explodes your family.

Wrenching
pain of death
ratchets relationship.
Loosen? Tighten?

Traumas,
magnifying glass,
enlarges tiny flaws.
Uncapped toothpaste tube
suddenly a gaping,
infected wound.
Anthill transforms
to craggy mountain.
Shivers above me
in an 8.5 earthquake.

Nothing
stays in balance,
the whole world reels.
Reference points vanish,

     s
       h
          a
             t
                 t

Staying   *e*
concurrent.

Impossible!   *r.*
   As we spin
      on a different axis,
         at different speeds,
           in different orbits
              of understanding.

Death's earthquake,
pain-filled tremors
jolt each partner's core,
sudden magma shifts
too deep to be detected.
Volcanoes erupt,
devastating
everyone
in sight.

We tried to go it
without help.

Please hear me.
"Get help – good help.
  It's there, reach out early."

Grief
seems
to separate,

men   and   women

parents   and   siblings.

Grieving
patterns
differ.

One mourns
while
one replaces,
one talks, one is silent
one detours, one encounters
one detaches, one connects.

People keep saying,
"But you have each other."

Oh, how little,
Oh, how little they know.

The things
one knows,
so deeply,
needs to talk about
are uncomfortable,
bring tears
or anger
in another.

For us,
listening to,
supporting Dawna,
the only aspect of our grief
we have done easily
together.

Hold on,
be flexible,
tolerant,

talk to each other,
give yourselves time,
there *will* be aftershocks.

Families,
marriages
that make it
are often stronger.

Fathers (Grandparents, Siblings and Partners, too)

I so often hear you asked,
"How's his Mom doing?"

As anguish challenges
your every moment.

So rarely,

"You are in my thoughts."

"How do you miss him most?"

"I remember him…"

You're so often ignored.

You have feelings, too.

Storm

Nothing
I say or do helps.
I watch in gathering panic.
Grief — a tornado — crashes
purpose, parenting-filled life.

Brews of darkness cross sunlight.
Numbness billows, as depression
distances into dank blank, chilled silence.
Tormenting memories block joyful ones,
swirls of redundant, raw, agonizing pain.

Blocked by our culture's pressure locks,
stone-grays churn with torrents,
yet only sprinkles come, no tears.
A howling Williwaw* lashes
isolated sullen sadness.

Friends and clients,
like birds, scatter to shelter,
disappear in this endless storm.
Phone reached-for remains undialed.
Office wall absorbs blank staring hours.

Concentration vanishes,
anguish erodes confidence.
Caged rage explodes as claps of thunder.
Lightning flashes in scary bolts of anger.
Meaning evaporates. Why work? Why live?

Time wanes long cold storm.
Blue sky — once again — yet,
still more clouds than before…
As sunlight breaks through our lonely storm,
will purpose again come to our hills and valley?

*An Alaskan Indian word for a violent wind-driven horizontal storm.

Siblings Always and Forever

So happy, so willful, so funny.
A sister, forever?

One day, her brother
her buddy died —
no good-bye,
I'll miss you,
I love you.

Will grieving parents,
once adventurous,
spicy-full of life,
abandon me
in their limp
sorrow?

Please not forever?

She's become a sad,
grief-insulated,
fearful, lonely
only child.

Will that fire of anger
at him for leaving,
always rage
inside her?

Please not forever?

Her peers' discomfort
emanates in hushed,
banishing voices,
ostracized.

Will our holidays
always be dreary,
meaning...
stolen?

Please not forever?

Glimpses of her wisdom,
compassion beyond her years,
give me hope that she will return
with her funny, happy, willful assurance.

She will know,
she is his sister.
He her brother, forever.

Teen-eggs

Grief at fifteen
seems beyond impossible.

As hard to sort out as yolk
from scrambled eggs slathered with
piquante hot chili salsa.

Teen egg whites are
a healthy challenge:
   questioning
    exploring
     playing
      joking.

  Yolk thick with insecurity
  vulnerable to fear, rage, sullenness.

  When broken,
  and whipped by grief,
  a two-colored egg
  changes
  to pale yellow.

        Then heated,
        with normal teenage
  Only tiny   steam and hormones,
  streaks of hope relieve that egg gets well cooked.
  all that yellow,
  almost total isolation:
    denial   Now cloaked
     nightmares   in sorrow's salsa;
      rejection   they deliver more jolt
       fearfulness than any Mom can stand,
        timidity. let alone a grieving one.

        This grief-scrambled,
         hot salsaed teen-egg,
         makes me wish
          I could reorder
          my teen-egg
           sunnyside-up.

Grandparents

Your Grandchild dead.

Your child an amputee,
not of limb but heart
maimed of purpose,
life's meaning
gone.

Your dreams,
your hopes,
your name
will not
live on.

Grandmother,
grandfather,
has anyone
recognized
your pain?

Masquerade

My old friend
Guilt,
masked,
is knocking
on my door.

Look.

Is guilt,
even
blame –
insecurity,
anxiety of
      lack,
        pain,
          attack,
            abandonment,
each fear in costume?

The imposter,
discovered,
cannot
stay.

When
I see fear
for what it is,
"Here he is, again."

Peace

comes
through
the door.

Guilt

skulks

away.

Angry

Why wasn't it me?

A child doesn't die

before

his
mother.

Abandoned.

Not once but twice.

Please honor
my

rage

with the dignity

it deserves.

Grief's Slug

Numb

blob

slug.

Barely

moves

on

tear

trail.

Sits.

Hardly

thinks.

Minute's

work

now

takes

weeks.

Living

hurts.

Let

me

die

too.

Out of My Body

When I start
a slide down
the mountain
into pain,
part of me
slips out
   above,
      beyond
        reach.

      Hovers.

    Watches.

Waits.

Returning

My soul,
my spirit
encounters
all lives, all time.

Recharged,
it returns refreshed
from floating free…
with wholeness and joy
beyond this life,
beyond any
one…
life.

I know
I am not my body.
I am free, as God created me.

Etched Words

A thousand times
I saw it at your waist.
Those words went unnoticed.

As I hold your buckle
even twisted and burned –
it tells your triumphant story.

"*Ride and Tie*"
"*Race Completed*,"
etched in bronze,
quietly speaks to me
of each day lived fully.

Life
for you was
"Ride and Tie."

You left
  no day,
    no relationship,
      no business unfinished,
        no loose ends untied.

Your race *was* completed.

Hatching

Yesterday
I held an egg.

A tiny chick
began pecking

slowly,

   slowly,

      slowly,

pecking its way out
of the shell
to set
itself
free.

Today,
I see…
each of us,
like the chick
inside the egg,
ready to emerge
free…

Why am I
so happy and excited
when a chick frees itself,
yet feel so abandoned
knowing that Derek
left his shell?

He left me
here
in my shell.

He is free.

I, too,
will hatch
before long.

The Seed

How does it know?

This little seed,
how does it know

to become
a weed,
a tree,
or
a rose?

How does it know?

Dawna Davies
(written at age 6)

Laughter

When my mind starts to wander,
the first thing I hear
is laughter.

Endless ripples,
like the water
in our creek.

I can hear their laughter –
brother and sister
partners
friends
as they throw meadow muffin frisbees at each other
    squirt each other in a milking "Star Wars"
    dive yelling into the cattle drinking hole
    run and splash in the sprinklers
    ride up the hill on the horses
    razz each other doing chores
    hunt frogs, turtles, crawdads
    fish in the creek
    build their "secret fort"
    share a picnic lunch
    play ball in the field
    bike to the beach
    read to each other
    tell great stories
    poke and fuss
    or sing in the car
    race when late for the school bus
      as their cows trot
        to the fence
       to say "hurry home,"

    or giggle in their room.

What's funny about a fart?

Yes, I hear their laughter…

Remembered Dinners

Two children,
eight and ten,
ask, "Can we invite
        company for dinner
           if we cook it?"

Each has specialties.
One dish,
maybe two,
but a whole meal?

That's this story.

Menu decisions:
        Color – red
          green
          yellow.

        Balance – bread and cereal
          milk and meat
           fruits and vegetables
         sweet for treat.

Four supply lists:
        garden
       freezer
      on hand
      market.

Who does what? When?
Clean up your own mess!!

What's for dinner?

Start with:
   Goat cheese they made themselves.
Dawna - Flaming spinach apple salad.
Derek - Pasta homemade! Fresh and tender.
Dawna - Roast pork from a pig they raised.
Dawna - Wheat bread, fresh from the oven.
Derek - Butter from our Jersey cow's cream,
              bright yellow, naturally.
Dawna - French beans, garden fresh
              with her hollandaise sauce.
Derek - Corn, run from the field to the kitchen.
Derek - Lemon pie, a mountain of meringue,
              ten home-grown egg whites tall.
              It looked like San Luis Peak,
              road and all.

The children had been
Mr. and Mrs. Madonna's
requested dinner guests
at their eclectic
Madonna Inn.

Turnabout.

There's no doubt,

Alex and Phyllis
will always remember
milking and chores,
then dinner on our farm.

Tears in Food

Food –
the store,
the kitchen,
the dining table –

where grief confronts me.

I hate to eat
   or
I binge.

I can't face the kitchen,
       once the heart of our home.
I'm in a trap –
      a cage of grief
         when I try to cook.

I sob.
I avoid
the store until
   there is absolutely nothing
     but mustard in the refrigerator,

       then

I cry up and down market aisles.
I weep inside
   while I try to eat,
     looking at
       the exquisite
        porcelain heart
          on our kitchen table,
            made in memory of him.
        It holds forget-me-nots.

For thirteen years
   Derek and food
     went together,
       nourishing us.

I miss his mischievousness.

I even miss the crawdads
   and fish from our creek
     startling me in the sink.

I miss his help.

I miss his going with me for groceries.
I miss his picking the salad
     from our garden.
I miss his pasta and the floury mess.
I miss his canning with all the family.
I miss his setting the table.
I miss his eating with us.

I *miss him*.

I don't cry so much now.

   I'm learning to serve
     food without tears.

Thank You

How did you
always remember
to say "Thank you"?

No matter how
small or large
the help we gave,
you made sure
we knew
it was appreciated.

Even as
a toddler,
it was
as if you knew
you might not have
the chance to say "tank oo"
again, another day.

Then
you grew tall –
so near a man –
yet all boy
and
still
so kind,
so thoughtful.

Of all those "Thank yous,"
the one
I miss,
remember most,
is "Thanks,
        Mom,
            for dinner.
                It tasted good…"
        as
            you
                touched
                    my
                        shoulder
                            softly.

The Ring

Just
weeks
before
his death,
he found a ring.

A ring
like ripples
in a stream of gold.

"Mom,
  would you
    wear this ring?"

He slipped
it on my finger
with "It looks like a mountain,
          with a hill and a valley.
          Just like life,
            isn't it,
              Mom?"

The ring fit perfectly.

Had an unknown jeweler made it for my finger?

Where did it come from?

It was just there on the dirt.

Derek,
  I thought
    you'd like to know.

I still wear the ring.

Your Rope

The only rope you left
is an old one
you didn't like.

You packed the rest.

Your bag disintegrated
with your body
in the crash.

That old rope
frames your photo, now.

When I look at it,
I feel
the harsh surprise
of the rope
on my legs
as you toss
practice loops.
Those loops annoyed me,
yet warmed my heart
with that pride
a mother feels.

I know you loved to rope.

I loved to watch you rope.

I can see you heel
  the sawhorse,
    dog,
      lambs,
        or
          heifers.

I often find
the rope encircling
this void inside and
my memories of you.
As I stand looking at it,
tears rope down my cheeks.

I know
you'd laugh
and say,
      "Oh, Mom."

Skip and Boots

Your old dog Skip is grayer now,
yet sturdy and staunch he stands.
Chore boots, cracked and weathered,
bid "Welcome home" from our porch.
Skip still barks as a plane flies over
as he did when you were here.

He was a cuddly fluff of a pup
when outgrown boots in the rack
were joined by those larger and new.
As the chore cycle closed,
racked and upended washed boots
stood drying and ready to wear.

Dawn's frost crystals crunch under boots
as when you and Skip walked to the barn.
His ears always lift at the drone
of a distant plane or of one drawing near.
The bark brings that thought.
Could he know a plane took you away?

Now your old dog Skip
lies among flowers graveside.
His crusted nose on his paw,
his eyes watch the porch
where your old chore boots
stand as dusty gray guards.

(Inspired from "The Steadfast Tin Soldier" by Hans Christian Andersen)

Farm "M's"

Music shared is magnified.
Music
on a family farm
may not mesh with milk
until you hear two children
singing Handel's "Messiah"
a cappella,
as they milk
their cows and goats.
A munching medley
with the metronome
of a milking machine
on a still moonlit morn.

The moos of cows
    mantras of pigs,
        goats,
            sheep,
            chickens,
        frogs from the creek
merge with mist
or muttering windmill,
        coyotes wail matins.

At times
you can hear
the moan of an oboe
meticulously playing
a modicum of Mozart.

Madrigals to barbershop,
"The Messiah" to country western,
show tunes to camp songs,
hymns of praise.
We sang them all.

Mozart Festival
each year, principal oboist
sponsored by two children
with their milking money.

Madrigals
Milk
Money
Mozart
Music
        Music
            Music...

Girls

Football,
roping cows,
horses,
even
your dog,
still came
before girls.

Yet
your head
turned
as they
walked by.

You enjoyed
their phoning you,
as girls now do.

We knew
some girls
had been
very
special,
too.

I smile
today,
motherly
judgment
suspends,
where once
I would have
frowned.
We found
two copies
of
Playboy
among
your treasures.

You

were

a thirteen-

year-old boy.

How Many Pretzels?

Remember dancing?

Four of us,
Dawna and you,
Dad and me

we danced
all kinds;
we liked
western dancing
best.
Not square dancing,
but western swing.

You and Dawna race
to finish milking
and other chores,
then race again,
"get ready quick
    we're going
        dancing."

I can still
smell
your Dad's
aftershave lotion
on you.

I can still
see
that freshly washed,
more than meticulously
combed hair,
such
a change from
the haystack
of blond straight hair
we usually saw you wear.

I can still
see
the two of you
dancing out
across the floor.

I loved to dance
with you,
but
even more,
I loved to watch you
dance with Dawna.

You learned to follow,
feel the rhythm.
Then to lead.

As you found the need,
you two learned,
then together taught,
       Swing
        10-Step
         27-Step
          Cowboy Two
           Schottische
            Texas Two-Step
             Cotton-Eyed-Joe
           Polka
            Windmill
             Windshield Wiper
           Yo-Yo
           Waltz
            Cuddle
            Freeze
             Cowboy Two
            Triple-Step
             Duck Under
             Deanna Lynn
             Cowboy Two, Again
             Aggie Stomp
             Triple-Step
             Shuffle Dance
              Two-Step Swing
                 yes,
              The Pretzel.

Remember the night you taught 80 couples to Pretzel?

Dancing in Boots

Over
the years
we danced
in the moonlight,
under the stars,
on polished dance floors,
in parking lots or patios,
even in the kitchen to the radio.

Smooth worn
leather soles
on cowboy boots
slid across those floors.
Even with heels on boots
your sun-streaked hair
barely topped my belt buckle
when we started to dance together.

Tall and short,
Dad and Dawna, you and I,
often caused a chuckle or two.

Your boots
always looked too big,
until

suddenly

after all those years

you were

as tall
as I.

Those 10½ boots
grounded you well
even at 5 feet 8.

It no longer
looked and felt
awkward to be held,
     twirled,
dipped, swung, spun,
    whirled away in your arms.

With hair
blown dry,
creased jeans,
polished boots,
you looked,
even smelled,
so near a man,
but still a boy,
my son.

Our son…

Though
Dad and I
loved to watch
you dance with Dawna,
I felt proud and pleased

when you'd coltishly
toss your head
and invite

"Mom, let's dance."

I'm sure you're still dancing.

Do you know
how I long to hear
those words
again?

"Mom, let's dance."

It's Your Birthday

February 5th

Dear Derek,

You
were born easily
fourteen years ago this evening.

I still smile
at the doctor's words:
"I love you farm girls.
   You come without fears,
      lie down and have a baby
         like the cows who taught you how."

         You
         came easily,
         lived easily,
         learned easily,
         loved easily,
         left easily.

         You
         touched in
         often enough;
         there could be
         no doubt you were real.
         You'd pester, taunt, tease Dawna
         as a brat, a boy, a little brother.

         You
         already
         understood so much.
         I often wondered,
         were you raising me?

You
met us,
taught us
on our ground,
not asking us
to come to yours.

You
always
seemed to know
where you were needed.

Were you meeting my needs,
while I thought
I was meeting yours?

You
were clear
on what was important,
adjusted your or our focus
as new light came into the picture,
like dawn into a new day.

You
knew
what was
right and wrong.
It seemed you brought it
with you from somewhere else,
used it here
most of the time.

Your
clarity
made you
determined,
difficult at times.
When I didn't understand,
you knew what was important.

Life forced few tears from you.

You
moved
cautiously,
rarely falling,
even as a toddler.
You'd just sit down gently.

You
understood
choice,
its role in life.

No need complaining.

Would
you still
be with us
had the pilots
heard you
as you often said,
"When I watch
       where
          I'm going
             I won't fall?"

You
mastered
the lessons
this life held.

Somehow
knowing this
makes it possible
to accept your flight…

Yes,
clarity,
caution,
thoughtfulness
were gifts you gave us
as your stream of life
blended with ours
for a while
and now flows on.

Lovingly and thankfully,

Mom

Note: *This letter was actually where I discovered writing would be a helpful healing tool for me. This was the first piece I wrote.*

Notes of remembering...

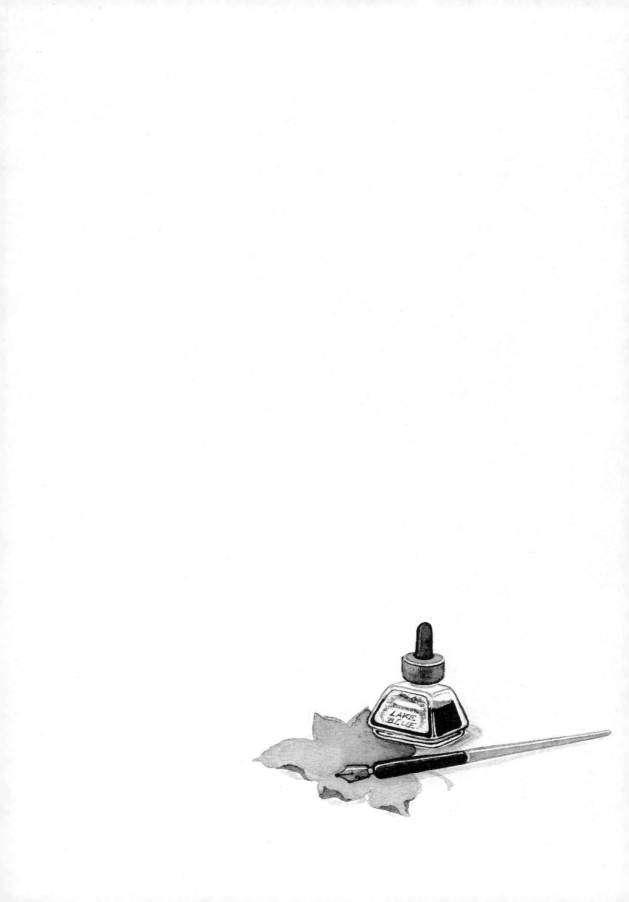

New Order

Suddenly
peak three
stands ahead of me.

Recognizing
the finality
in a fatality
slowly joins
new expression,
inconsistently
moving toward
reconnecting,
re-entry.

Watch out.

An avalanche breaks loose.
Jolting vivid recollections
knock me down, but
do not crush me.

Where will I get
the energy to go on?

Painful flashbacks
punctuate evolving order.
Reorganization appears
as we work our way
up and over
summit
three.

Four steps forward,
one or maybe five back,
yet reinvolvement comes.

Grief's Lights

Light,
  the sun,
    the moon,
      the stars,
change how I see.

Light can blind me.

Grief blinds me.

At first
that's all I see.
Then grief
changed how
and what I saw.

Its floodlight
shone directly
in my face.

Now
it follows me
    stalks me
      taunts me.

I can no more
run from grief
than stop sunlight
    moonlight
      starlight.

Even man-made
lights follow me
haunt me.

Car lights.
  Firelights.
    Candlelights.
      Beacon lights.

Neon lights
on and off
flash
waves
of grief.

The rheostat
of time
slowly
dims
grief's rays.

Airplane lights,
even
airplane sounds
once unnoticed
now surround,
terrorize.

Now those
  lights expand
    my range of vision.

No escape,

everywhere I go,
they hum like bees.
They look like birds by day,
by night like stars.

They've profoundly
  changed how
    and what I see.

Who escapes?

Seasons on Our Hills

Halt
my hurry,
tune into life.
At points of change,
even points of pain,
find new depth of meaning.

Against
our changing hills
time and life
feel fragile
now.

Winter's
tune of rain
dances a jig
on our trailer roof
road washes out,
our bridge underwater.

Then new grass jumps
overnight from dampened soil.
A lush fairyland
of green velvet carpet
drapes the shoulders
of our Irish Hills.

So vivid,
my breath stolen –
Can this be real?

I pinch myself.
Is this Heaven?

Spring
wind-spun
windmill.
Water fills
gray tanks
on the hill
sloshes over,
cascading a waterfall.

Tears
fall as I recall
years I watched
from our kitchen window
as I made cheese, butter or dinner
while he ran across those pastures
with his sister, as day turned dusk,
their dog, calves, goats and kids
frolicking behind.

Tender green
crescendoes
into a symphony,
vibrantly performed
in blue
    lavender
      magenta
        rose
          yellow
            poppy-gold
wildflowers on the slopes.

Summer
hills turn amber.
Breeze pulses
its soft rock song
on grass and croplands.
Fields of grain wave,
a gentle reminder
of Derek's
wind-tousled
blond hair.

Autumn's
endless rhythms,
harvest sounds:
grinding grain
snapping beans
shucking corn
chopping stalks
whirring fruit dryer
simmering apple butter
boiling canning kettle
popping lids.

To remind me
even on a farm,
there should be
time for resting,
the hills take on
that patina of age,
the gray-brown hue
of time and weather
on an unpainted barn.

Unharvested seeds fall,
on sun-drenched soil
waiting for rain.

Between
autumn and winter
slips in a tender season.

Holiday's
earthbound stars
color the hillsides,
bring joy and heartache.
Lights, like twinkling jewels,
shine through my longing tears.

Memories
jolt me painfully,
then cradle me as I cry.
With passing time
tears are both
the dew of pain
and
pearls
of remembrance.

Our hills
share their
changing melodies.
The seasons remind me
change has purpose,
is valuable,
recognized,
shared.

Back-to-School Night

A few moments
on the high school campus,
I'm screaming inside in anguish.

What's happening to me?

Everyone
is laughing,
     talking,
          saying "Hello."

No one else
sees or feels

torturous explosions,

flashing neon lights of anger
in pitch-dark night?

Dreams
shattered,
burned with your body,
when two airplanes
collided, crashed
just a year ago.

But dreams of this year
slipped by me unnoticed,
then jumped out of the dark

     screaming.

"Why aren't you here?"

Derek, this was the year.
Dawna's senior year.
Your freshman year.

You and she
were more than anxious
to be in school together,
after five whole years
in separate schools.

Finally, together
in school one last year.

Years of walking
running
or biking
to the school bus
were going to end.

Dawna is driving now.
You two, *driving*.
On your own.
Independent,
talking,
laughing,
best friends,
sharing secrets,
business partners,
dancing partners,
brother and sister.

I didn't realize
the together dreams
were living on... band,
                    choir
                    tours,
             stage choir,
          double-dating,
         youth symphony,
   international jazz festival,
football, basketball, baseball games,
livestock shows, fairs and rodeos...

It's Back-to-School Night.

You're supposed to be here, *Derek*.

A *Problem*

The toughest time?

Christmas night.

I saw it coming.

If Christmas Day
is a tricky wrinkle,
by Christmas evening
it is bound to be
a sticky wicket.

"Please come over."

You are welcome
at our Open House;
dessert, singing, sharing.
Bring your honest
gift of sadness
and at least one
beautiful Christmas memory
to bare and share together.

You'll have a Christmas
worth remembering
when you discover
Christmas
in your heart.

Christmas,
once known,
must be rediscovered.
A birth,
life begins again today,
each day,
each Christmas.

Now Christmas evening,
sharing,
caring with others
is that pleasant
          laughing
                    cheerful heart
of our Christmas.

Not a problem,

Christmas.

Waiting

Why can't I stop

looking
at the sky...

watching
for the door...

listening
for your footsteps...

waiting
for your voice
      smile
        or touch?

How
many times
does my heart
have to flare with joy?
I see you,

then

      it

             falls,
s
  h
    a
      t
        t
          e
           r
on the floor   *e*
             d

when I find he's not you.

Mother's Day Bouquet

I see you
across the room,
down in the field,
roping in the arena,
running along the beach,
in a movie in the theater,
biking along country roads,
blond hair tousled by the wind,
even wearing the jacket
you wore *that* day...

Sometimes
you are a little boy,
oftentimes a teen,
at times a man.
Yet always
our son.

It's

you

coming
down the street,
the Mother's Day
bouquet in hand,

the dozen
yellow roses
you so proudly
brought to me
this day last year.

I still can't believe
you are not coming home.

Today is Mother's Day.

Time

Derek's
death

   stopped me,

made me
 look
  at
   time.

When
 what
  I feel
   I need to do
    doesn't fit in,

I need to ask myself

why
 I need
  to do it.

Often
 I find
  if I let
   someone
    else do it

I meet their needs.

Not Getting Lost

I must
learn to live
without seeing you.

Coping with
just one moment,
one hour,
one day,
helps me not get lost
as I learn to live again.

Are my
choices today
in line with
a lifetime
of love and peace?

Seven
balance points.
Each is important,
even in life's worst traumas.

I thought you'd like to know,
"*Living Intentionally*,"
  the course we organized,
    taught as a family team,
      still works for me.

Seven areas –
Choices *written*
assist me
find clarity,
keep balance,
as I spin, swirl, reel,
engulfed in traumatic growth.

SPIRITUAL

Leaps in understanding
  come with study, prayer and thought.
  Refreshing. Renewing.
  The lesson, Sunday.
  The "Daily Word."
  The "Course,"
  my quiet time.
I begin again each week, each day,
  sometimes each breath – heartbeat.

FAMILY

It's hard
  learning to be
  three, no longer four.
  We're making it slowly,
  with difficulties at times.

We backpacked through snow
  on the Pacific Crest Trail
  to Uncle Patt's camp last week.
You would have loved that trip
  Yosemite, once again.

PHYSICAL

Exercise,
  vitamins,
  good diet,
  enough rest,
  recognizing anger,
  acknowledging stress,
  venting grief with writing;
  help me stay in good health.

PERSONAL

Pleasures
  just for me;
  taking classes,
  breaking a colt,
  working at the ranch,
  redoing my wardrobe,
  changing my hair style,
  reading a book a month,
  letting go of my fears of writing.
Learning to set boundaries.

PROFESSIONAL

Keeping in touch
  with pulse points
  of my work
  requires constant effort.
No new projects, thank you.

HOME
>Think in terms of one day,
>>one hour,
>>one moment
>>>rather than a week or month.

>Sometimes
>>all I can handle
>>are five-minute blocks of time.
>>>Five minutes:
>>>>dust,
>>>>water plants,
>>>>make a salad,
>>>>Set the table,
>>>>wash one window,
>>>>clean the bathroom,
>>>>straighten the living room,
>>>>unload-reload the dishwasher.

>A calm, inspiring home still takes effort.
>The new house you wanted
>>to help build is coming along.
>Our farm is simplified,
>>we can almost handle it without you.

SOCIAL
>Helping others with grief
>>challenges me to grow.
>We're still dancing,
>>though short a partner.
>I speak often about WORLD NEIGHBORS
>and Third World development.

Choices
written out in all seven areas
each month,
>checked each week,
steady me.

A sense of balance
>allows me to not get lost
>>this most difficult year of my life,
my first year without you.

A *Filly*
and
Wranglers

I washed
your new Wranglers
the day you flew.

Those 27 x 34's,
now faded
to blue-bonnett blue.
The filly and I
have nearly worn
them out for you.

One day a week.
Thursday, the day
I save to be with her,
         with you.

We do the things
you and I love so much:
gather cattle off the hills,
bring in cows and calves,
sort and doctor,
work the chute.

I started her at two.
Now she's "com'n three."
Light, quick and easy
as we work those cows.
She trots to the gate
when she hears me
call across the field.

She's a dream come true.
Your Dad gave her to me
for our nineteenth
wedding anniversary.

Even faded blue
Wranglers and a filly
bring an important
spot of balance
in my life.
As I adjust
to not seeing you.

Celebrating Seasons

For years
on season's change
we have stopped and
shared with others.

We have potluck parties.
Friends from across the fence
and around the world
gather in our living room.

From their scrapbook of memories
each shares verbally or through music
a glimpse of the coming season.

Without celebrating,
seasons can blend,
  spring into
    summer,
     autumn,
      winter,
all unnoticed.

Another year

whooshed by me.

Take note.
Find
most life responds
   to the sun,
     to the earth's tilt.

Celebrate the change with us.
What does the new season mean?

Bring two things:
a dish towards dinner
and a poem,
    object,
     song,
      or your thoughts
       of the coming season...

Summer
may mean
sandals,
endless energy,
long lazy days,
sweat on brow,
a zucchini explosion
if the seeds you plant
number more than one.

Autumn
nippy air,
school begins,
golden pumpkins,
silver queen corn,
butterflies come home
to the eucalyptus grove.

Winter
snowfall,
ice crunching
chilly chores,
holiday hustle,
quiet contemplation.

Spring
greening hills,
those daffodils
my mother calls
"telephones to God."

We remember,
see, hear, feel,
differently.
Words, music, sharing
widen our vista.

Friends come
whose homeland
has two seasons
instead of four:
wet and dry,
food and famine.

The angle
of the sun
on our world
brings more change
than we often recognize.

Though you've gone on,
We still celebrate seasons.

Investing in Memories

Every moment holds a memory.

Remember…
each evening
during dinner
we passed verbal photos
of each other's day.

What do you want
to remember about today?
What lessons did life teach you?

Keeping tuned to each other.
Living with antennae
turned to *now*,
shared.

Recalling laughter and tears.
Vignettes, vivid snapshots
of the adventures of your days,
our "*scrapbooks*" are full
of memories of you.

Remember…
the sweat on your brow
as you pushed the bus out of mud
on wind-swept Andean mountain roads.
At 14,000 feet above the level of the sea,
in oxygen-thin air you helped
a Quechua village farmer.
A glimpse into his life –
the immense
challenges
he faces.

Home again,
apprehension,
then smiles and laughter
as you taught other children
to milk your goats and cows.

Playing football
with your heart and soul;
the amazement on your face
when they named you
"*Player of the Year*."

Walt Woodard's shock
was matched only by your own
as you caught on the third go-round
to win your first three-steer roping.

Those wonder-filled three months
we took you both out of school
to trace, see, touch and taste
our roots across this land.
We each became
part of our nation's history.
We found her grandeur,
her pulsing pride,
her fragility.
Plaguing problems came into focus.

Flying into an Eskimo village
over backs of moose
browsing on snowy tundra
slid time back half a century.
Grandpa and Grandma taught here
on this wilderness edge of the world.

Pulling those defying weeds,
planting innumerable seeds
persistently with Grandma
in the warming soil and sun.
Selling produce we didn't need
from the back of our old
'55 Ford pickup truck.

The tension and concern
etched your face as you helped
one of your and Dawna's cows
give birth on a cold, stormy night.

The thrill of climbing through
the mist along the Inca Trail
to find ancient mystery
in Machu Picchu.

Memories to remember...

Bedtime, talks with God,
those special, private talks.
What shall we thank Him for tonight?

Remembering...

You invested in life each day.
You lived more fully in thirteen years
than many people do in a *lifetime*;
partially, because we as a family
invested in memories.

Derek, we still do.

You Made a Difference

You saw,
  understood,
        believed,
            made a difference, Derek.

Throughout your thirteen years
you watched WORLD NEIGHBORS*
help our friends,
most of whom we've never met,
have more food,
clean water,
better health,
grow three bags of beans
where only one grew before,
in some cases ten bags instead of one,
because their village asked
WORLD NEIGHBORS' help.

In millions of villages
in still-developing nations
across our earth,
mothers,
fathers,
children
need to learn
to care for their land,
to nurse it carefully,
enabling it to produce
ample food to feed
their families.

They know
their land, climate, traditions.
They want to solve their problems.

We work together,
not doing things for them
and not giving things away
but blending old with new ways,
discovering seed that grows.
Most of all, we watch them see
a new vision of themselves
as they teach their neighbors
what we've learned together
for sustainable change.

You understood
the careful tending it takes
to get poor land
to produce
strong
crops.

In the years
you lived with us
you touched more lives
than we realized.

In fact
people are
still donating to
WORLD NEIGHBORS
in memory of you,
Derek,
to help continue
the quiet assistance,
creating positive,
appreciated change
in remote villages
across our world.

In death
your love,
your concern
for others

continues…

Derek,
you are still
making
a difference.

Note: WORLD NEIGHBORS *is a nonsectarian international, private, volunteer organization which accepts no government funding. For more information:*

WORLD NEIGHBORS ♦ 4127 N. W. 122nd St. ♦ Oklahoma City, OK 73112

We Saw

hopeless,
gentle people.
Quiet valleys.
Steep hillsides
slashed and burned.
Eroding, tired soil.
Poor crops.
Endless
poverty,
hunger.

Cities call
a better life
jobs – money.
Villagers go.
Hope soon turns
to desperation
in degrading
demeaning
slums.

Then
we watched
WORLD NEIGHBORS
inspire discouraged families
to rebuild barren soil.
Simple methods
experimenting
starting slowly
starting small.
Villagers
instruct
other
villagers.

Many
slum dwellers
return to family
farm with dignity.
Resourcefulness,
enlightened
enthusiasm.
Prosperous
valleys
we saw.

Today

Can I use
my anger
my pain
as impetus
to tackle
to challenge
and to change
intolerable wrongs?

Can I use
my moments
my hours
to help others
to soften pain
to find their feelings?

I need to leave
a gentler
healthier
more
loving world.

When my time
like yours
Derek
is up.

Why Did I Wait So Long?

Why did I think I couldn't write?

Writing,
always difficult,
always filled with failure,

until…

Through foggy numbness,
it came cascading,
as water slips over
the waterfall
into an inlet
in a Mirror Lake.
Refreshing
misting spray,
those relieving tears,
discovered rainbows.

Writing
now lets me play
with words and sounds.

It's a positive way
to pull myself into
a reflective,
sheltered
bay.

Idea,
question,
pondered,
held,
a nascent spring
once locked in rock.

I have something to say.

Writing
settles thoughts;
s
 e
  d i m
       e
         n
          t
                 f
                  a
                   l
                    l
                     s,

Writing
and water
clarify,
expose depth,
reveal unknown dimensions,
as crystal returns light
while passing it on.

                        d
                         r
                          i
                           f
                            t
                             s

Unneeded,
a word let go
is not loss.

                               a
                                w
                                  a
                                   y.

Crisp.
Strong.

Even here,
as everywhere,
a teaspoon given
returns
as a cup,
a bucket.

Overflowing...

Why did I wait so long?

Releasing, I receive.

Message "swiftens"
by honing the flow.
Its meaning has
more edge.

Writing and water
carve into the cliffs of time.

Alone

Today
being alone
is almost sacred.

As morning breaks to dawn,
snuggle into the comfortable chair.
The warmth and crackle of the fireplace
stir new understanding…

With the coming light of day
the big black glob
in the living room window
slowly transforms into
a majestic mountain.

Oaks,
rocks,
the deer grazing
come into focus
as concepts and thoughts
take on clarity and form.

Somehow
this is best done alone.

Tears come most easily alone.

Peace and joy
are decisions
I make

alone.

Choice

Standing surrounded
by loving people,
I am lonely.

Surprised, I find
I make this choice.

I choose

to feel sorry for myself
as a victim of life and death
                or
to help others understand
and grow through their griefs,

to complain of Dawna's
messy room and unmade bed
                or
to appreciate the blessing
she is in my life,

to see you critically stare
at the scar on my face
            or
to feel your wonder
at who is behind
my deep blue eyes.

to think sad thoughts
of missing Derek
            or
to think happy thoughts
remembering the years
we shared,

to call for love
        or
to be loving.

I find
  warmth,
    security
      in seeing
        aloneness as
          just one
            of my choices.

Sticky Mud

To keep
even
one foot
in the stream
requires all,
every tiny ounce,
of everything
I can muster.

One foot
stuck in
the sticky
mud of grief.

It is work
to free myself
by not resisting.

Shift energy.
  Shift weight.
    Shift thoughts.
      Shift perspective.

On more solid footing,
the sticky mud washes off
as I participate
I wade toward
life again.

Trees and People

I heard the whisper
of wind in the trees
in this sun-filled meadow.

It said,
"Trees are people."

Trees
stand tall,
usually in couples
or in families,
branches touching.
Yet others stand
by themselves, alone.

Trees
lean on those
around them when ill
or uprooted by a storm.

Trees die.

Trees
must get
a message
their time here
has come to a close.
Notice
even they
have a sense of urgency
to leave a mark on time.

A dying pine has a thousand cones.

Trees
experience
transition, death.
Trees have another lifetime.
They burn as light and warmth.
Cut down, they stand again
in barns and buildings.
After all,
they turn once more
into the ever-nurtured land.

"Trees have several lifetimes."
"Trees are people."

I heard this from the wind.

Our Understanding Garden

As we walk through life
at points of lessons,
there are joy, pain.

We stop,
     watch,
          feel.

When
we look,
we always find
a flower growing.

Flowers share
their understanding:
seeds, bulbs and cuttings.

Understanding,
comes home
with us.

In our valley,
there's a knoll
on the sunny bank
along the creek
where Grandma planted
   "trees of wisdom."

Flowers grow
among those trees.
Seeds tended lovingly.

Come…

sit,
share,
or read.
I am often here.
Derek is here.

Come…

pick a bouquet
in passing, as you leave.

Notes on emerging order…

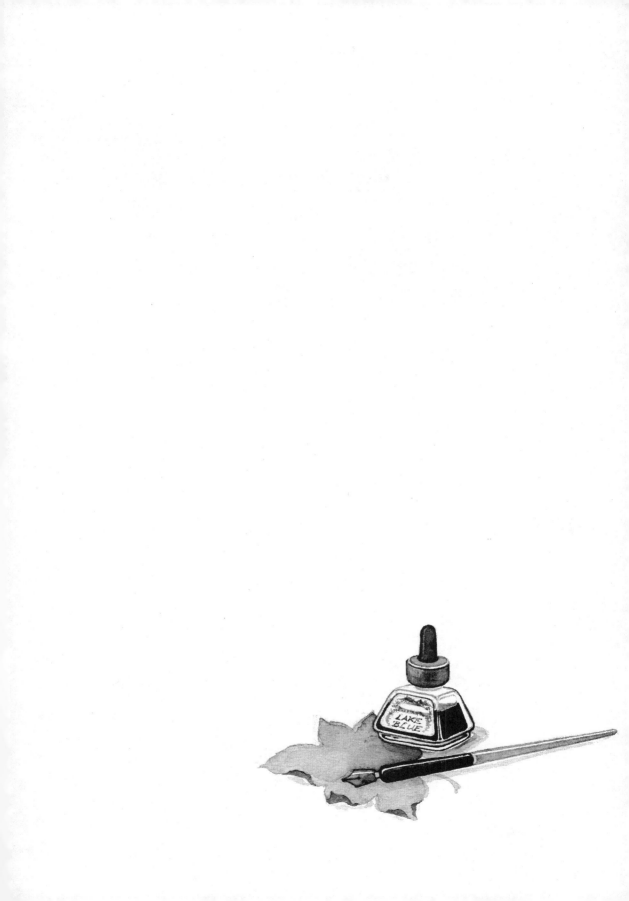

Perspective

*4*th

It happens.
No struggle.

Life

finds me

as I descend
from rugged peaks
to this breeze-rumpled rise
of pastures strewn
with flowers
not seen before.

Examined
wild blooms
hold answers to
my question,

"Why?"

A new vision
of myself emerges
as I leave these mountains.

Above the Fog

He learned easily,
not needing to climb
the garbage heap
of mistakes
and
unlearning
as most
of us do.

Did he bring the wisdom
of many lifetimes
when he came
to live
with us?

Clarity,
    a gift he gave,
        a gift of good-bye.

I need to use it.

When I do,

I stand

on a mountain
above the fog,

seeing

forever.

His Mother and Me

When
I stay
tuned to
my whole self,

I feel
no sense
of separation
from Derek.

Only
when I
separate myself
into

his mother

and

me,

do I find

pain and sadness.

Our Pendulum

Shock
of insight
showers me.

I
 s e e

  we swing

 between

   two points

loving
  and
   calling help!!

 Peace
    or
      pain

  it's a choice.

    Nurture – accept
     or swing to
     calls for love.

    Illness, guilt –
    see,
      hear,
        feel
    their root in fear;
    pain, anger, hate,
    jealousy, even crime.
    Are these calls for love?

    Can
    I shift
    the shape
    of my response?

Love is comfortable.

Comfort knows.

Is that the meaning
in timeless words?
"Love is patient and kind,
    does not demand its own way
    goes on forever..."

Little calls still call.

Life,
people,
nations,
our world
looks different
when labels
good — bad
are replaced by
caring and fearing
    or
loving and calling for love.

I

s   g

w   n

i

My
choice,

a caring perspective
or
staying in my own call for love.

My perception shifts,
    swing from
    calls for love
       to
        loving.

No mystery.
Simple miracles.
The ill become well.
Fear dissolves in love.
Life moves to unseen.

Is that what He was saying?

Listening

"Why
   haven't
      I written
         more of anger,
            when Anger's
               gnaw
                  is often
                     relentless
                        in grief?"

When Anger
comes to visit,
I may yell and scream.

Eventually
sitting down,
I'll listen,
looking
at my thoughts.

"Anger
   resisted
      is enticed,
         empowered,
            as are
               those other
                  calls for love:
                     bitterness,
                        complaints,
                           fear and pain."

"Isn't compassion loving listening?"

When
Anger
comes by,
I welcome her,
listen to
his call for love,
compassionately.

Lost?

A friend
        said "Hello" today.

As we stopped
        and talked,
        she said,
        "I'm so sorry
                you lost
                        your son."

I smiled,
        saying,
                "Thank you."

I feel warmed,
        cared for
        when someone
        remembers you,
        Derek,
        and says
        your name.

Then I thought:

I miss you
        more than
        words can say,

                but the word   *lost*

doesn't fit.

You were
        never
                lost in life.

Why would we think of you as lost now?

Hillside Rock

Between garden and sea,
a rock outcropping,
a Madonna and child.

Nature-sculpted cliffs
on wooded hillside
bless his grave.

At times,
I forget him
for a while;

it's then I realize
she's still there,
in prayer.

Each Time

plane lifts into sky,
your message to Dawna
encircles me,
assures me.

"Don't be afraid to fly.
I'm flying with you."
Encircling me.
Touching me.

I am blessed.
An angel's hand,
a soul across time
warms my shoulder.

12

Only Twelve

Mother once told me.

"Remember,

childhood
is only
twelve
years
wide."

Yet,
my
child
is mine
forever
and *never*.

Show Me

Mom,
I want to know.
I need to know.

Just

show me,
show me how.

What's Important?

Cub Scout badges
sewn on by a boy
may not be even.

A sleeping bag bed
made up by a child
may have a wrinkle.

Christmas gift aprons
sewn by youngsters
will not have a label.

Children-owned animals
cared for and loved
may be a motley lot.

Ledger and bank book
kept by a small boy and girl
may not be bookkeeper neat.

One step to success
then another, another –
enthusiasm builds on itself.

Salad, pasta or pie
may not be perfectly made,
yet what is really important?

Fear and Parenting

Parenting
is not
protecting
but
loving,
preparing
our children
to be independent,
unbound from our
limiting dreams and fears.

Free to
contribute
to our world.

Not knowing
what, where or how
their unique
contribution
will be made.

In constant
amazement,
we encourage
awareness as
our children
explore.

In wonderment
we watch them grow
through their choices
and also, ours.

We are still learning
to ask ourselves,
"Are we saying
   no or yes
     because of fear?"

"Is fear a call for love?"

"Is love letting go of fear?"

"Is parenting loving
     as we let go of fear?"

How Long?

My friend,
I understand
the sight of me
brings thoughts
you find hard
to comprehend.

I see our pain.
I feel our fear.

Could it happen?

Yes,
it could.
And if it did,
you would survive
and come to know
my yearning.

Please see me
as just a friend.

How long must I
understand?

Only One Person

Only
one person
ever told me
they recognized you,
Derek, as I did.

"He is an angel."
Those four words
told the story to my soul.

That instant bond
to another lifetime
etched in my memory.
Written in a neon tube
across a moonless midnight sky.

Now, another life
is being knowingly blessed
by your gentle mature soul.

Across Lifetimes

In awe
I watched.

I felt it.
I saw the light,
their faces, resplendent
as He
confirmed
souls touching –
as mother and child.

It
was
months
before
I understood
the commitment
made that day.

I am privileged.
I am a witness.
Awe-filled.

Child Light

The peace
and light of God
are shining on us now.

I watch our children
they too are light.

How do you touch
a moonbeam,
lightning,
a soft glow,
sunlight?

Watch,
enjoy
the
splendor.

Dawna,
witty and thoughtful.
An independent moonbeam,
sparkling, laughing, dancing
across this meadow of my life.
Yet at times
a bolt of lightning,
surge of thunder,
cutting through
what stands
in her way —
a disquieting storm.

Dylan,
stillborn,
our unknown son,
is a gentle
loving
glow.

Derek,
who moved
on at thirteen,
is sunlight smiling
on my meadow.
His mellow
consistency
smooth,
warming,
resonant
as dawns
and sunsets.

The peace
and light of God
shine in me now.

Una Melagro Pequeño

Perception shifts.
That's a miracle.
Una melagro pequeño.
Spring focuses on the now.

Flowers, leaves, songs of birds
burst forth with the joy of the moment.

    Spring sings, "Rewaken."

"Look
  smell
    feel
      remember.

Memories are part
  of who we are today."

    Spring eloquently touches me.

It helps me
  reach out in love,
    even when I'm hurting.
      Sharing love and caring
      softens my pain,
        brings joy,
          courage to others.

    Spring gives life to what looked dead.

Life was there
  unseen
    in leafless
      trees.

    Spring brings a timeless cycle of renewal.

It lets me know
  life goes on
    for those we love
      yet cannot see.

My Stream

My rivulet began
on a drizzle-soaked
grassy slope.

A thin stream
glistens in the sun,
I wander down the hillside

trickles
flatten
into puddles
of childhood
resting, growing.

Youth's
storms
over-fill
my pond.

Suddenly
unbound
I race
fearless,
down rapids,
boulders,
waterfalls,
white water,
endless energy.

Joy – leaping.
Pain – falling.
Why waste time
in backwaters or eddies
when I can shoot rapids.

Cutting
into the brae,
currents pull me
into the mainstream.

I carve cliffs,
flood fields,
rip out
fences.

Mistakes
dam up
as lessons
still unlearned?
Misjudgments,
no isolated incidents,
no unconnected instances?

Lost
and
holding
in brackish
backwater.

I recall holding
causes blockage,
ultimately pain,
I let go.

Days,
months and years
tumble over
the spillway together.

I want
to dance
over rocks
around trees
along my banks.

It's hard to
learn to drift.

Then
one day
I slow,
fascinated,
a gentle eddy
roving clouds.
I float in the sun.

Sharing,
merging
my rhythm with
those coming toward me.
I'm drawn to some currents,
avoid or enfold others
longingly,
linger,
love...

Here
I recall
no life
no water
no matter
no energy
is ever lost.
Doesn't it all recycle?

Accepting what
comes,
you and I, my friends,
flow together
then apart,
yet still
connect.

I am
with you
as far as you
allow my current
to go with you.

Please use
your current
to carry me
when I need rest,
or

you may
leave me
for a while
as you flow on
or

race
past me
to the sea,
learning lessons
more quickly than I.

I will

   slowly,

     painfully,

fill

  the

    space

     you left.

When I go
as far as I can,
I wait quietly
for the renewing current
of life's next
experience.

I merge
with others
in a family of streams,
deepen,

then I begin to slow.
I'm drawn to
meander,
as flow gentles.

The ocean
ultimately calls
my stream.

Will my water
evaporate to clouds,

then rain,
another lifetime?

Reservations

Living,
we soon forget
we are only
lent
to this world.

Our sons,
our daughters,
in fact all of us,
come with reservations
for a flight
to another experience.

No one-way tickets are issued.

To Another Mother

Growing through our pain may be
the most courageous thing
we ever do.

Some things are
as clear
as rain-washed air
to me,
strange
as they may seem
to you.

That's all right.

We each choose
our own path
through
grief.

Reaching out
to you
helps me.

I hope
it will
help you.

Life's School

Were the world
a perfect place,
where would my soul
go to school?

This community
we call our earth
holds relationships
and experiences
from which I learn.

Are we in this world confused
as to why we're here?
We cry, hide or scream,
calling out for the love
we must learn to *give*.

As we learn to live and be,
why is it so hard to see
each other and ourselves
as God sees us,
created perfectly?

It seems this life
we've known
is a grade
in school.

Homework

My soul has homework.
What must I learn today?
Lessons toward enlightenment
often come in strange ways.

I know I am part of the peace,
the light that's here.
Yet I ignore it, crumple it,
even start to toss it away,
then ask, "When will it come?"

Deep down, I know the peace;
the light is here today.
I trap it in limited vision.
I refuse to see my illusion.

Like the tree I think I see,
then chemistry shows it
again multidimensionally
in elements and atoms.

Who is the teacher?

It's you.   It's me.

How and When?

QUICK

Is exit quickly
the choice
some of us
make?

Do we need
to be here
longer?

Are those
we leave
strong enough
to learn
without us here?

DOORS

Does
death have
two doors:

"Quick"
and
"Linger?"

Before
we die
does
our soul
commune
on the door
through
which we pass?

LINGER

Do
some
choose
the door
marked
"Linger?"

Do we
need to stay
awhile,
let go slowly?

Will
an illness
give us time
to resolve
relationships,
express feelings,
help us and
others learn
release?

SLEEPING

Why can't we all
go quickly
and
quietly
in our sleep?

VIOLENT

Why is quick death
sometimes
violent?

Did it feel like
a dive into
an icy lake
to
Derek?

STILLBIRTH

Do some souls
turn
before coming
through
life's door?

Do they
choose
not to enroll?

Did our stillborn baby,
Dylan,
only need
our love
and
his experience
within my womb?

Was
something
completed
that set
him free?

SUICIDE

Did my friend
who took
his own life
show me
anguish,
possibly
poor choice,
inner strife,
his
restlessness
needed
a new beginning?

Was it an anxious
call for love
we ultimately
discover within?

Can I see him
as a soul
now freed?

Another chance?

Will he
re-enroll
for
unlearned
lessons?

Can his
curriculum
be less
frustrating?

BODY

Is this body
just
clothing
our soul
wears?

BEGIN or END

Is death
an

ending
or
beginning?

Are there
lessons for all
when lives touch?

"Are you ready?"
or
"Do you need
to stay awhile?"

In lingering
can we
slow or speed
the growth
of others and ourselves?

STILL HERE

It often seems
the gentle souls
go first,
the ones
our world
needs most?

Have they
learned
their lessons?

Do those of us
who cry
need to realize
we may have
more
to learn?

Macramé

Families,
organic
free-form,
ever-changing
fabric sculptures.

Ours
closely woven,
blue, purple,
pink, turquoise
flares of brilliance.

One day

the turquoise strand –
we cherished,
    depended on,
was
            jerked out…

ripped from our weaving.

Three
strands
now build
our tapestry
instead of four.

At each
contact
where the turquoise
would have touched
the purple,
    blue
  and
pink – maturing to rose,
the pattern changes.

Each strand
must choose again –
leave a gap or cling closer.

At first our weaving
shuttled faster than
before,
events and decisions
made together.

Then
our crafting
lost its rhythm

gaping

           holes
sag
   g
    g
     g
       in sadness.

The fabric weakens.

Four fibers weave
three braid,
two twist
when one stands

        a p art

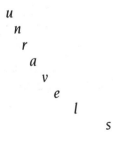

            alone.

Now,
tighter
maybe even
tighter than before.
Its twisted
   braided
    latticed web
much altered.

Tears, time,
light of death,
have blanched each
brashly vivid strand
a mellowed hue,
still woven.

My Notebook

lets me
be a mother.
It's part of me.
I hold it
on my lap, in my arms,
or it sits beside me.

As a friend,
like no one else,
it says
back to me
those names
I long to hear.
It lets me
talk, cry or laugh,
then cry, again and again
if I need to.
It doesn't leave
    as Dylan did,
        as Derek did.

Like a teacher
it lets me
look, feel, then grow
into a new freedom
with and from
the past.

My notebook
absorbs my anguish,
        my pennings,
           my trickling thoughts,
                my raging rivers of remembrance,
                    my awakening awareness.
My child.
    My friend.
      My teacher.

I hope you have a notebook.

Good Morning, Son

You died over a year ago,
though
you're
not gone.

As Dawna says,
"Derek
  is with us
    wherever we go,
      even when
        we can't see him."

Good morning, Derek,

I need to thank you
for allowing
a portion
of your spirit
to walk,
    work,
      write,
        be
with me today.

New Direction

In our forest garden
near the creek
or on a hilltop;
I untangle.

Verve
transforms
to lassitude,
shifts to vision.

Inner sight,
  intersight,
    insight

unfetters
energy
from
confusion,
clutter,

released
to purpose.

My perspective changes...

5th

Refocus

Do I really
  want
to give up
the security
of my grief?

It's become a familiar,
almost, comfortable place.

I'm not sure.

Yet I need to
see life clearly
once again,
refocus.

Anger,
sorrow –
  vividly
    painful
      memories –
slowly shift
and fade
into a softened
blurring background.

Dusk moves into twilight.
Grief turns reluctantly
as night reconciles,
envisions dawn.

Acknowledging
his death,
this new day.

I stroll
slowly
carefully
across this knoll.

I know
my grief
has and will
soften over time.

Refocus.
  Redream.
    Resolve,
I *am* living again.

Now

I realize
more than before

each moment,
family
and
life
are
so
fragile.

Savor today.
  Smell it.
    Taste it.
      Touch it.
      Feel.

Light it with
redreaming,
  caring,
    seeing,
      being
        love.

Now will be *gone* tomorrow.

Forever Free

What's left to fear?

Some whose trek
climbs through grief
toward understanding
accept the gift
of being
forever
free of fear.

We struggle,
         survive,
                  discover.

Those who go on
are not just
the body we knew.
They, too,
are more than seen.

As I grow through
the greatest fear
life can offer,

I have nothing
left to fear.

I am free.

Possibly,

forever

free.

Pasture Gate

Yesterday
my refocus came.

Standing
talking with him
at our pasture gate

I felt
the lens turn.

The past shifted
toward a blur,
the future
began to
clear.

Derek,
"I must
   let you go.
      I'm needed here,
         I have growing —
            helping yet to do."

His smile confirmed it.

As if his work was finished.

"Ride on across the pasture.
   Ride on to what you must do.
      Ride on, my son.
         Ride on."

An ending.
A beginning.

My refocus came at a pasture gate.

Three Messengers

An Easter lily,
nearly forgotten
on the porch,
resprouted,
then grew.

Months ago
the lilies
bloomed,
but this one
had something
on its mind,
a timing
all its own.

Two years ago
today
we last saw
your smile.

On the porch,
radiant
in three
full blooms,
the lily
greeted me
this

August
morn.

A New Day

Over these
two years my grief
softened ~ blurred.

Today at dawn
the lens moved, again
now clearer ~ crisper.

Refocused on tomorrow.

I said
"Good morning, Son,"

"Good morning, World."

I have faced your death.
I talk with you.

I see
that part of me,
   that part of you,
      which floats free.

When I need you,
and take time to listen,
your advice comes in clear.

I now understand;
you needed
to go on.

I am no longer angry
you left me here.

Refocus
doesn't mean
erasing or forgetting
but reinvesting in life.

It's being freed
of that throbbing pain,
guilt, sorrow, regret
of raw grieving.

Yet grief does not die.
Still I sometimes cry
with gentle, lonely pain.

I'm still here.
I have growing,
helping yet to do.

Most often, you will find me
smiling with happiness
and warm deep joy
as I think of you.

Reconciled,
I knew you,
I *know you*
as my son.

My

New

Ruler

Measure
for my days

— Questions —

clear my path.

Is it an adventure?

Is it healthy for our world?

Does it help someone?

Is it fun?

If not,
why
should I do it?

I like my new ruler.

Ever One?

Aren't
they,
He,
you and I
ever one?

My Kayak I

At dawn,
together
with
my kayak
of quiet time,

I ask for
adventure,
balance, stamina,
courage and clarity.

This vision
steadies me
down creek
to lake or open sea.

We glide
ripples, rapids,
even storm swells.

Again, at dusk,
in quiet time,
cares and negatives
drift past to the sea.

In starlight,
serenity
refocuses
to gratitude,
gentle, grace-filled joy.

My Kayak II

Dawn,
in kayak
quiet time.

I ask
balance,
stamina.

I explore
creek, lake,
river or sea.

I glide,
ride rapids,
storm swells.

Dusk
quiet time,
cares drift past.

Starlight, serenity, joy.

I...

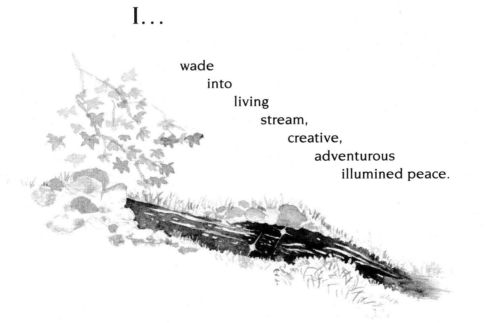

wade
    into
       living
          stream,
             creative,
                adventurous
                    illumined peace.

Notes on refocusing...

To Help Me - To Help You

At this point the reader will find a shift from the more poetic pieces.
Here begins the clearly poetically formatted prose, followed by checklists
and other self-help materials. They are an abrupt change, yet they are an
integral part of the growth I experienced. This collection of information was
prepared for our family use and has been included because others have
found the same items helpful. Acknowledgments are noted with an * and
source information is given on pages 314-315.

The transcription of the memorial service is titled *"Our Good-bye"* and
relates the experience in poetically formatted prose as if it were written to
Derek. This piece has been meaningful for many people who were present,
as well as for those who were unable to participate in this memorable
experience.

"How You Can Help?" answers a frequent question. This section recalls
the images of how people helped our family grapple with the deaths of two
children. These pieces were included to help others see how they can be of
assistance when faced with the question, "What can I do to help a grieving
person or family?" There is a more formalized list beginning on page 277.

NEWSPAPER ARTICLES: The reprint of two newspaper stories which
appeared at the time of Derek's death gives an editor's and a news reporter's
perspective of him and our family.

Our Good-bye

Derek,
it feels important
to share your memorial service.

August 29,
five days after you died.

We were the ones
who had to do it.
The three of us.

No one else
knew you
as we did.

We thought
we had said
"good-bye"
to you, Derek.

Yet,
in letting
you go in love
rather than in anger,
we find
we've said

"Hello"
to you
at each new turn,
each new day
in our lives.

I know you were there that day
though we couldn't see you.

Remember,

morning light
beamed through
the stained-glass windows,
blessed the flowers,
then flooded on to touch
each person in the church.

Mrs. Thomson,
your piano teacher,
played Bach's
"Jesu', Joy of Man's Desiring,"
the notes soaring tenderly.

The church wasn't large enough.
Many stood or sat outside.

As I looked out
across that audience,
my mind registered each face.

I realized
the diversity of the world
in the friends who said
by their presence
they too would
miss you.

How had a boy
of thirteen years
touched so many lives?

To open the service,
we - your father, mother and sister -
stood together in front of the altar
while your Dad prayerfully
shared the thoughts
the three of us had
earlier that morning,
the fifth day
after
you died.

"Dear Father,

*We join together
in memory of Derek
and of all others who have passed
from this physical existence.*

*Our family
and those here
and those who have
sent messages to us
from around the world
feel Your comfort and Your love.*

*We pray
that our friends who mourn today
might know that same comfort.*

*Please hold
them in Your arms, Lord.
Heal them of grief,
sorrow, anger, fear and regret.*

*Our faith in You is our strength.
All is well with You at our side.*

*Through this experience of losing a child,
help us all find Your gifts
of joy, peace, love, hope and rest.*

*Lead us into new pastures of awareness,
nourish us with the full dimension
of Your spirit
so we can each renew
our commitment
to life.*

Amen."

Suzan Boatman
walked forward to sing
"You'll Never Walk Alone"

It was the song Auntie Pat
had sung at our wedding
as Dad and I began our walk
in life together.

It's a song the four of us,
you and Dawna, Dad and I,
sang often.

You'll Never Walk Alone *

When you walk through a storm,
hold your head up high,
and don't be afraid of the dark.
At the end of the storm is a golden sky
and the sweet silver song of a lark.

Walk on through the wind,
walk on through the rain,
though your dreams be tossed and blown.
Walk on, walk on, with hope in your heart
and you'll never walk alone.
You'll never walk alone.

Uncle Patt
stood next to speak.

You were going to spend
a week's vacation
with him at the ranch
when you took off in that airplane.

He mentioned
that his heart went out especially
to the young men
and women, your friends,
who were struggling
to accept your death.

He could hardly speak,
and even in his pain,
he reached out
to comfort others.

Tears moistened eyes.

"Derek had an uncanny
ability to be friends
with people of all ages.
One of his very special friends
was his grandmother.
They spent hours,
literally weeks, working
in the garden together.
Derek understood how
to help things grow.

Another special friend
was Rebecca,
a little girl,
one year old.
When together,
their eyes
were lit with joy.

Derek was friends
with all of us.

Like myself,
I see men out there
who saw him as their own son.

I feel a great gratitude
in my heart towards
Bill, Phyllis and Dawna
for sharing Derek
with us freely.

Sharing a child
makes that child somehow bigger;
they have more and more love to give.

Derek grew like that.
He affected all of us.
Everyone who ever knew him,
even for a short time,
remembers him.

People who saw him years ago,
even before he could go to school,
working with me in the mountains,
stop even now and ask,
'How's your little nephew?'
I tell them:
'He's not so little anymore.
He's growing like a weed.
He's just as nice.'

Derek had
a wisdom about him.
We all recognized that.
A quiet wisdom.

There is a story I'd like to tell:

One time
Phyllis ran a red light.
Derek was in the back seat,
barely two years old.
Just beginning to talk.
Phyllis was busy driving along.
She didn't notice
a policeman
pulled up behind her,
lights flashing,
but no siren.
Derek reached up
and tapped her
shoulder.

'Moma, I's tinks uoos has a poblem.'

Derek's
gentle countenance
will stand close to us,
will live with all of us forever.

There is a poem I'd like to read.
It says the author is unknown.
But after you have read it once,
you will know the heart
of its author,
probably
as well as anyone
can know another person.

A Child Is Loaned *

I'll lend you for a little time
a child of mine, He said.
For you to love the while he lives
and mourn for when he's dead.
It may be six or seven years,
or thirty-two or three,
But will you, till I call him back,
take care of him for me?
He'll bring his charms to gladden you.
Should his stay be brief, you'll have
his lovely memories as solace for your grief.
I cannot promise he will stay,
since all from earth return.
There are lessons taught
I want this child to learn.
I've looked this wide world over
in my search for teachers true,
From the throngs that crowd life's lanes,
I have selected you.

He selected Bill, Phyllis and every one of you.

Now will you
give him all your love,
nor think the labor vain,
when I come to call
and take him back again?
I fancied that I heard them say,

'Dear Lord, Thy will be done.
For all the joy Thy child shall bring
the risk of grief we'll run.
We'll shelter him with tenderness,
we'll love him while we may.
And for all the happiness we've known,
forever grateful stay.
Should the angels call for him
much sooner than we've planned,
we'll brave the bitter grief that comes,
and try to understand.' "

After Uncle Patt finished,
your sister,
Dawna,

with poise and composure
that belied her fifteen years,
walked to the lectern and shared:

"'Simple Gifts'
was a special song
to Derek and me.

In a lot of ways
Derek was so simple;
he had enough of everything
and more to share with everyone else.

He sang the solo in this song
with his junior high school choir this spring.

I'd like to share some of the words with you:

> 'Tis a gift to be simple.
> 'Tis a gift to be free.
> 'Tis a gift to be gentle.
> Tis a gift to be fair.
> Tis a gift to wake
> and breathe the morning air.
> And every day to walk
> in the path we choose
> is a gift we pray
> we may never
> come to lose."

She then walked to where the choir was standing.

The choir loft was filled to overflowing
with your friends from school, Derek.

They sang the song again, for you.

This time
it was Dawna
who stepped out
in front of the choir
and sang your solo.

Simple Gifts

'Tis a gift to be simple.
  'Tis a gift to be free.
    'Tis a gift to come down where we ought to be.
And when we find ourselves in the place just right,
we'll be in the valley of love and delight.

  When true simplicity is gained,
to bow and to bend we shan't be ashamed.
To turn, turn will be our delight,
'til by turning, turning
we come 'round right.

'Tis a gift to be gentle.
  'Tis a gift to be fair.
    'Tis a gift to wake and breathe the morning air.
And every day to walk in the path we choose
is the gift that we pray we may ne'er come to lose.

Tis a gift to be simple.
  'Tis a gift to be free, free, free.

Traditional Shaker Hymn

Your Dad
then walked to the lectern.

"It is a gift to be free.
That's the relationship
I tried to have with Derek.
I didn't want him to take hold
of my fears and prejudices.

I wanted him to be free.
Free to move beyond…

Three things come to mind
that I want to share with you,
because there are so many lessons
I learned from him.
I just can't hold them back.
They need to be shared.

I worked with Derek in conquering fear…

When we first moved
to our place,
There was a clump of trees,
kind of a thicket.
He was afraid
to go down there
at five years old,
even in the daylight.

It wasn't long before
he had cleared the whole thicket.

I remember
the last time
he reached for my hand.

Many parents
remember that moment.
Realizing a milestone has passed,
we wait for the next time,
but it doesn't happen
again.

I remember that time.

In Peru last April,
we were hiking from
the Inca ruins of Machu Picchu.
Derek wanted to explore all the trails.

The picture of Derek
on the memorial card
I took at Machu Picchu.
I really took the picture
because I wanted to remember
the carved stairs of the Inca Trail.
I asked him to sit on the rock.
I didn't realize why
I was taking
the picture.

One trail was sufficiently dangerous,
the group had been cautioned
not to climb it.

You can guess
whose fear kept us
from climbing that trail.
It wasn't Derek's, it was mine.
We climbed the easy trails.
That's where I took the picture
that you are holding in your hand.

I watched Derek develop love. . .

   I don't know
that I helped
him much on that one.

He did that himself.

He loved all the animals
at the place, each one.

I can't tell you
how much he loved
his friends in 4-H.
Many of you were
with him two weeks ago
as you stayed with your animals
at the county fair.

He loved each person in his family.

He loved music.

Occasionally, I'd take him
to barbershop chorus practice.

One of the last songs
we were learning,
the Pacific Express Quartet sings it,

'Everybody Wants To Go To Heaven
But Nobody Wants To Die'

He sang lead in that song.

He loved dancing, riding,
sharing his experiences
with all of us.

The joy of this last summer
was beyond what
he had ever known.

That's why we feel that
his time had come.

I don't think he had a sad moment
this whole past summer.
He did everything
he wanted to do.

The third thing I want to share is that he had hopes...
    He had overcome a fear of flying
and was anxious to become a pilot
as soon as he was old enough.

He long ago learned to drive
and drove his old pickup
all over the property.
It seemed a long time
before he would be
        sixteen.

We were starting
to think of a motorcycle trip
across Australia in about two years.

The trip I had taken years ago.

He couldn't wait
to buy a horse for roping.

He was anxious
to continue with music –
piano, oboe and singing –
expressing himself
in those ways.

And . . .
I can never remember a time
when I did something for him,
no matter how small
that he didn't say

"thank you."

I can't say the same thing.

My hope for all of you is –
    That you can conquer fear.
    That this experience
        may help you conquer fears.
    That you can develop love.
        I know you have
        because we have felt it.
        We feel it now.
    You have hopes and dreams.
    Let this be the first day
        of the rest of your life.

The trip to Peru
was with people interested
in an organization called
World Neighbors.

Bill and Lila Yeager were
with us on that trip
and are here today.
We have asked
Bill to share."

Bill walked to the lectern.

"All of us on the trip
to Peru were there to see
the results of World Neighbors'
efforts in that area
of the world.

We are an organization
of concerned people,
helping people
learn to help
themselves.

As we met Derek,
the first word
that came to our minds
was that he seemed
to be such a 'shining' person.

It was interesting
to see how comfortable
he was with adults.

The two Davies youngsters
were the only children on the trip.
They both fit in very quickly.

He seemed to love nature
and the out-of-doors.
He went out of his way
to be friendly and helpful.

The most memorable part
of the trip was the Altiplano.
This high country is very remote.
The roads were extremely
steep and treacherous.
It seemed we were
getting out of the bus constantly
to push out of the ruts and mud
ponds that formed in the road
during the rainy season
that had just passed.

The most exciting part of the whole trip
was to see what had actually happened
in the villages where WORLD NEIGHBORS
had been assisting.

In one of these remote high communities
at about 14,000 feet in elevation,
in an effort
to thank us
for the changes
that had occurred,
the villagers met us
in traditional costumes
with dancers and musicians.

We followed them along a little path.
They showed us the increased crops,
their experimental plots
and their improved livestock.
At the community hut we saw
the handcrafts the women had made.
They showed us the ways
in which nutrition, sanitation and health
of the people in the village improved since
WORLD NEIGHBORS had come to help them - help themselves.

Derek had brought
one of his ropes along.
On the way back to the bus
I watched him show the villagers
some tricks with the rope,
to everyone's delight.

Another memorable moment
was when the chiefs and mayor
of an adjoining village
came to ask WORLD NEIGHBORS
to come to their village
to help them accomplish
the same improvements
they had been watching occur
in the neighboring community.

These people were discovering
what Derek already
knew about life and agriculture.

There is great value
in gentle loving care,
in the helping of people,
in the care of land,
in the opportunity to introduce them
to appropriate locally available technology,
which helps them learn to experience success.

Derek understood agriculture because that was his industry.

He paid his own way on that trip.
That would not have been possible
had it not been for Dawna and Derek's
enterprising efforts.

In that regard we have much in common.
WORLD NEIGHBORS' goal is not to do for people,
but help them discover the thrill of success
as they learn how to solve their own problems.

    Later today we will pick up our lives.
We are going to go back to doing
our own things, in our own way.
But we will take Derek's light
and example with us,
in our minds,
in our hearts.

He knew,
he always knew
there was work to do,
some of it God's work.
He knew that there were
many truths to be discovered,
that there were many to befriend,
few to serve.

And so be it."

For four days
there had been
so many people,
phone calls and decisions,
I had not found a quiet moment
to prepare what I would say
at your memorial service,
until after the service actually began.

Standing at the pulpit,
I was aware of the calmness,
the peace I felt – even though
I had never before spoken
to an audience of 700 people.

"There have been
only two times in my life
when I have felt
so held and so loved as I have
in these last few days.

I want
to tell you
about the other time.

It was when
I was giving birth to Derek.
We chose to have
no one else with us
during that process
until the very
last
moment.

Bill was with me.
I remember feeling
as if I were suspended
on a cloud of love.

I have absolutely
no recollection of pain,
with no medication –
just hard work,
joy and love.

That is what I have felt these days,

because you
and other friends
all around the world
have heard of Derek's death,
have come, have cared, have called
or sent your prayers
to support us.

I want to thank you all
from the bottom of my heart
for letting me experience
this joy and love one more time.

I feel privileged
to have known Derek
as well and
for as long
as I knew him.

We live life very fully.
We have no regrets.

Each of you
knew Derek
in some special way,
because Derek
was somehow able to meet
each of us where we were
and experience life
in the dimensions
that we understood.
He rarely imposed
another side
of himself
on us.

Those of you
who heard him sing,
or sang with him,
never saw him milk
at 4:30 in the morning
when it was cold and dark.
He didn't particularly
like the dark.

He went out there anyway.

Those animals needed care.
It was Derek's time to do it.

People who
saw him western dancing,
never saw him milk.

You who danced with him,
or whom he taught how to dance,
may not have seen him in school
where he was on the Honor Roll.

Some of you attended our goals class
the four of us occasionally taught,
called '*Living Intentionally*.'
Derek knew how to do that
very, very well.

Some of you knew
him as a businessman.
Let me tell you,
he watched his pennies.
Those of you who bought eggs from him,
beef, something from the garden,
or had dealings with him
in his investment program
with real estate,
never saw him rope.

Derek,
in his
thirteen years
of living with us,
lived more
than many people
live in a lifetime.

He was always happy.
He was always smiling,
all of you remember his smile.

More than any other comment
that people made about him to me
has been regarding his smile.

He always seemed to be happy.

You know,
most of all,
he always knew
where he was needed.

I deeply know,
Derek was needed
on that airplane.

As he boarded that airplane,
he was the happiest kid
in the whole world
when I hugged
him good-bye
and waved.

He was going to the ranch.
He was going to rope.

He wouldn't have
to rope on foot anymore.
He would have a horse to ride.

He had been out there
chasing the lambs.
He gave up
on the cattle because
they got smart after awhile
and could get away from him.
If he could get the lambs
in a small enough area,
he could catch them on foot.

When all else failed,
he would rope
the sawhorse.

The last things
Derek put in his suitcase
were his ropes
and a book.

A book called 'Why We Win,' written by
World's Champion Team Roper, Walt Woodard.

Walt came today
to share with you
the Derek that he knew."

Walt speaks of his experiences last spring.

"I knew Derek a lot different than most of you did.

He came to a Roping School that I had.

His mother was working
the catch pen, taking off ropes.

I thought that
it would be fun for Derek to catch,
then go down and visit with his mother.

But the one thing Derek had to do was catch a steer.

I thought, 'That's going to be my goal while I'm here.
I want that boy to catch a steer by one foot,
then go down there and have a celebration
with his mother.'

But when he rode into that arena
on a horse that he had borrowed
from Alex Madonna,
his stirrups were too long;
he was bouncing.

I thought, 'Oh, my God.'

He listened to what I said
and followed the words
right to the note.
He improved.

I thought, 'If he can't ride well,
it's going to be tough.

The first night he did well;
the next night he did a little better.
He heard some mention of a jackpot
with all the students
the last night.

He asked me if anybody could get in the contest.

I thought, 'Son!'

But said,
'All you need is a dollar and a big heart.'
He had a big heart.
He got in the contest.
I was hoping
he would catch the first one
and go down to that catch pen.

He caught the first one.
He went down to the catch pen.
I thought, 'Now that's one.'

His mother took his rope off the steer's leg.

He came back,
and he caught the next steer.
He made it to the finals.
It was a three-steer contest.

The last steer.
I thought, 'There's just no way.'
He roped the steer, and he won the contest.

When he did,
the first thing
that came to my mind was

'God, what a teacher I am!'

I know that I've said
the same things to 500 kids every year,
but not one of them has ever done what he did.

I'll always remember the heart that he had,
the things that he accomplished –
And that smile.

When they came and told me
that the plane had crashed,
I thought of something I had heard.
'We all came from somewhere,
and we're going someplace.'

The builder of the universe
didn't create this as a stairway to nowhere.

I'll see him someday. I'll be there.
I hope he doesn't keep practicing,
because when I get there
I'll be in trouble."

Then
Bill, Dawna and I
stood together and
invited everyone present
to come out to our place for lunch.
We assured them there would be plenty of food.

Bill then introduced John-David.

    "John-David Webster
is a special friend of ours.
Has led the music
at several CFO retreats we've attended.
We've been together singing many times."

John-David explained that the words to the songs
we would be singing were inside the Memorial Card.

He then added,
"We have all had the privilege
of knowing Derek in various ways.

If you are like me,
you've had the sense of
'I wish I had known him better.'

Indeed, we'll have that opportunity…

But now
we can at least know him
in the essence and spirit that were his.
These songs were selected with that in mind –
that we might know him and experience
the real essence of his philosophy,
his thinking and his spirit.

We'll begin with the first song."

Life is for Living *

Life is for living,
    whatever you will live for
    you will give.
Life is for giving,
    whatever you will give
    to life will live.
Life is for doing,
    for living, giving, doing,
    learning how.
Life is for you,
    and life is for me.
Life is for living now!

Life is for loving,
    whatever you will love
    enough is yours.
Life is for sharing,
    whatever you will share
    with others grows.
Life is for being,
    for loving, sharing, being,
    learning how.
Life is for you,
    and life is for me.
Life is for living now!
    Life is for living now!

"The family want you to have these songs,
in your hearts and minds.
Now that you've had a chance to rehearse,
let me really see and hear you
sing it like you mean it."

It was sung
with real gusto
the second time,
Derek.

"Freely, freely you have received. Freely, freely give."

Freely, Freely*

God gave me love in Jesus' name
I've been born in Jesus' name
And in Jesus' name I come to you
To share His love
as He told me to.

He said,
'Freely, freely you have received,
Freely, freely give.
Go in my name
and because you believe,
others will know that I live.'

All power is given in Jesus' name
In earth and heaven in Jesus' name
And in Jesus' name I come to you
To share His power
as He told me to.

He said,
'Freely, freely you have received.
Freely, freely give.
Go in my name
and because you believe,
others will know that I live.'

"Bind us together,
bind us together,
with cords that cannot be broken…

Bind us together with love.

If you would like to, reach out and touch someone."

Everyone joined hands.

Bind Us Together*

Bind us together Lord,
    bind us together with cords
    that cannot be broken.
Bind us together Lord
    bind us together
    bind us together with love.

There is only one God
    there is only one King
    there is only one Body
    that is why we sing.

Bind us together Lord
    bind us together with cords
    that cannot be broken.
Bind us together Lord
    bind us together
    bind us together with love.

"Let us conclude in that same atmosphere.

Let there be peace on earth and let
it begin with me."

Let There Be Peace*

Let there be Peace on Earth,
    And let it begin with me.
Let there be Peace on Earth,
    The peace that was meant to be.
With God as our Father (Mother),
    Family all are we.
Let us walk with each other,
    In perfect Harmony.
Let Peace begin with me,
Let this be the moment now.
    With every breath I take,
Let this be my joyful vow –
    To take each moment
    and live each moment
    in peace eternally.
Let there be Peace on Earth,
    and let it begin with me.

Amen

We invited
everyone again.
"Please come for lunch,
we need each one of you."

The TV news that evening reported that
between 300 and 400 people came to share
in the abundant food and visiting at our place.

Derek,
the memorial service
is how we thought we had said "good-bye."

Notes of remembering . . .

Derek 'had already lived a lifetime'

By Susan Seager
Staff Writer

At 13, Derek Davies already had a very definite course mapped our for his life.

The San Luis Obispo boy's goals for the year were to grow 4 inches taller, buy a home computer and a horse, learn to rope, get good grades and create a "calm, inspiring atmosphere" at home, according to a page-long list he made every year.

A more distant goal was to parlay the 12 head of cattle he owned with his 15-year-old sister, Dawna, into a ranch of his own.

But shortly after he got on Wings West Flight 628 Friday morning, Derek's goals were cut short when the passenger airplane collided with a small private plane. Derek was killed, together with the 12 other passengers, two crewmen and two men flying the single-engine plane.

Phyllis and William Davies lost their second son in that crash just 10 miles from their farm; Dawna lost her brother, only living sibling and best friend.

Between answering phone calls from friends and relatives, the three Davies sat in their comfortably furnished mobile home and talked about the blond, blue-eyed teen-ager who seemed to be filled with endless energy.

Two days after hearing the news of his death, the closely knit, religious family is teary but calm.

"Not one of us has a regret for things not done," said Phyllis. "Derek lived a very, very full life. Most people, in their full lives, don't do as much. He had already lived a lifetime."

Derek smiled often but was quiet and wise, his mother said. "It's as if I raised my grandfather," said Phyllis in a soft voice. "You just can't be sad (if) you knew him." To hear his family tell it, Derek never had a wasted, idle moment.

On the last day of his life, Derek was on his way to visit his two uncles on their ranch in rugged Alturas where he hoped to practice his newly learned skill of roping.

"There never was a boy who was more excited to get on a plane," said Phyllis. According to his sister, Dawna, "He loved to fly."

Tragically, Phyllis had made a reservation for Derek on an earlier flight, but decided against putting him on that flight because he needed his sleep and more time to pack.

But Phyllis said there was a finality to Derek's leaving that she has only begun to understand. He wrote thank-you notes to those who helped him at the county fair, where he showed his prize-winning pigs with Edna Valley 4-H Club. The notes should arrive in the mail today, she said. He also cleaned up his room and vacuumed the house, even though it wasn't his turn.

Derek Davies

And he only gave his mother enough money for three tickets to a barbecue all four Davies planned to attend. "He should have given me $24, he only gave me $20. He said, "That's all you'll need for the tickets."

Derek had worked hard all summer, milking his cows and goats, making and selling goat cheese and saving his earnings. He sold one of the pigs, the 220-pound Zardeo, for about $580 at the close of the fair.

He had paid for his Wings West ticket himself, drawing from his ample bank account.

He was hoping to shine up his newly learned roping skills at his uncle's ranch. He packed two ropes and a book by his hero, Walt Woodard. "I'll bet he read that book 25 times," his mother said.

His father took him to see Woodard perform at the county fair earlier this month.

He was to return after a 10-day trip to visit his uncles and prepare to start eighth grade at Laguna Junior High School, where he played the saxophone, oboe and piano, and sometimes sang solos for the Laguna choir.

Derek would probably have gone to Cal Poly (his parent's alma mater), Bill said.

Derek and Dawna shared household chores and profits from their goat cheese and vegetable garden, putting most into a savings account. Both agreed to tithe 10 percent of their earnings to the family church and World Neighbors.

The pair relied on each other for friendship at their isolated home, sharing a room all their lives. Now Dawna can't bear to sleep in the room alone. "She stays with us," her father said softly.

Phyllis was the last to see Derek alive. Their visit on the way to the airport remains clearly etched in her mind. As her son stood to board the plane, Phyllis hugged him and asked for a kiss. "He said, "Oh no, not here Mom,' and he gave me another hug," she recalled. "Then he walked through the boarding gate with a big smile. He turned and waved to me, she continued, her voice slightly broken.

"Father Al (Simon of the Old Mission Church) said, 'And he was already flying.'"

Memorial Services for Derek will be held at 11 a.m. Wednesday at the United Methodist Church in San Luis Obispo. The Davies family will officiate.

Derek's cremated remains will be buried at the family ranch.

Donations may be sent to World Neighbors, 4127 NW 122 Street, Oklahoma City, Oklahoma 73120.

In addition to his sister Dawna and parents, Phyllis and William Davies, Derek is survived by two uncles, Patrick Armstrong of Bishop, and Wesley Armstrong of Aluras; one aunt, Patricia Norris of East Windsor, N.J.; four grandparents, Philip and Jeannette Armstrong of San Luis Obispo, Ione Davies Isham of San Luis Obispo and Glenn Davies of Camarillo.

Editor's Report

By Michael Wecksler

I was sitting on my porch Sunday afternoon, reading the paper and watching the cumulus clouds roll overhead. It had rained the night before, and the smell, and the feel of the air made me think it would rain again.

I was glancing at the front page when my eye caught a story about a plane wreck in San Luis Obispo, which I consider my home town.

I read the story quickly, hoping not to find a familiar name, but I did.

It hit me like an electrical shock; young Derek Davies had died in the plane wreck.

I hadn't known Derek long, but I knew him well.

I lived in a trailer for over a year on the Davies' farm. I helped milk the cows, feed the chickens and till the garden. Once I even helped cowboy-Derek rope his silly dog Skipper.

Derek and I played together, and worked together every day. Sometimes we hunted crawdads in the creek, once or twice we rode our bicycles to the beach; in short we were buddies.

I called him "Sprout" – from the Jolly Green Giant commercial I guess – and it seemed appropriate; it was only a matter of time until he would sprout into a fine young man.

At 12 he could do the work of a grown man, and he knew things that take most of us many years to learn.

In fact, Derek was such a precocious child I often wondered who was the adult in our relationship.

I finally figured out it was him.

I hadn't seen Derek in over a year; once I left the farm I never visited again. I ran into his mother in San Luis Obispo from time to time, and she would tell me to go and see the kids, Derek and his sister Dawna. She told me how much they missed me, and they wanted me to visit, but I never found the time.

I guess that's the point of all this; I wish I had seen Derek at least one more time.

Most of us are pretty busy. It's easy to get tied up with your family and career, it's not always easy to keep up with friends, but we should try.

We live in a world where there are no set answers, no guarantees, and at any moment things can change drastically, as they have for the Davies family.

In one of his songs James Taylor sings "shower the people you love with love." What he's saying is if you care about someone let him know.

The world wouldn't change if I had seen Derek one more time, he'd still be dead, and I'd still be 500 miles away, thinking of him.

But if I had seen Sprout one more time I would feel a heck of a lot better today.

How You Can Help?

What is helpful in grief? Though I cannot speak for other families, I can tell you what was helpful and meaningful to me and to our family.

As I look back across this period of time, an increasing number of thought-filled and casual actions – even awkward moments – warmingly come to mind. In *It's OK To Ask* and *Two Long Walks* I relate some of these experiences. I have made an effort to thank those who helped us. However, this gives me another opportunity to say thank you. You will possibly be surprised to find yourself in this nameless list.

You will find other lists between *pages* 277-283 and blank pages included to jot notes of ideas which occur to you. These pages may be helpful personally and as you reach out to assist others.

It's OK To Ask

It did
throw me off
at first
when people asked,

"How are you doing?"

"I don't know.
   I'm still alive,
      I guess."

Now
I cherish
"How are you doing?"

followed by
a pause.

They listen.

It tells me
someone cares,
still remembers him.

"How are you doing?"

then
listening.

Your
listening
brings relief,
a warm, grateful
smile slips across my
face,
into my life.

Two Long Walks

Our two walks
along grief's way
have great contrast . . .

When our
first son died,
not a single card.
Outside the family,
not even the doctor or a nurse.
No one said, "I'm sorry.
       I know it hurts
         to lose a child."

      Young,
      in a city,
      working and in school,
      less faith in God.

      That time
      we walked and cried
      along the road of grief,
      alone.

      When Derek died,
      people in our small town
      and from across the world
      reached out to us with
      "I need to help you if I can.
       I'm hurting too."

Each tear,
each prayer,
each thought-filled
letter,
poem,
song,
card,
plant,
flower,
phone call,
dish of food…

people who
found courage
to drive out and see us,
willing to risk
facing their own
emotion as well as ours…

Each was important.
 Each is remembered:

 A young man
 we barely knew
 came out our long dirt road,
 not knowing what he would find,
 knowing only that he needed to come.
 He looked alone and scared,
 a bunch of home-grown roses
 clutched in his fist as he approached.
 He recalled he had talked with Derek only once.
 After a comforting visit,
 he left with a smile on his face.
 He had new understanding of himself,
 his own courage, and grief.

 The 4-H Club
 came out
 the day before
 the memorial service.
 A giant vacuum cleaner
 swept over the farm.
 Children, teens and parents
 with rakes, pitchforks and brooms,
 cleaned corrals, barn, shed, water troughs;
 picked produce, weeded gardens, and mowed lawns.
 They brought dinner – hot dogs, buns and marshmallows –
 to cook over a campfire.

Each was important.
  Each is remembered:

Those who found the time
to come to the memorial service,
to share in lunch after the service.

My mind, like a camera,
took a picture of each person.
It was then I discovered
it is more important
than I ever dreamed
to attend services.

The spotless kitchen
greeted me
as I went into the house
late that afternoon
after all those friends
who came had been amply fed. .

A farmer we'd never met
sent $50 with his card:
"There will be
    unexpected expenses.
      I know, I
          lost my wife."

Someone came by
with toilet paper,
Kleenex™ and
vitamins –
they knew . . .

Each is remembered:

Songs,
concerts,
performances,
the 4-H yearbook
were dedicated
in memory of Derek.

Editorials,
Letters to the Editor,
people from across the country
sent us news stories
that mentioned him.

Peace Corps friends
heard his name on a radio
in the heart of Africa,
then walked all day to call.

Several people
called and asked, "How can I help?"
Each came out, and as we visited
they helped me clean cupboards,
                closets,
              windows,
        straighten the books,
          weed the garden,
            pick produce
              and can.

Two mothers
I had seen in town
and at school functions phoned.
"Would you like help decorating?"

For that holiday I couldn't face!!

Our home had never looked "so like Christmas."
We used the favorite family ornaments,
lots of ribbon, lights, and angels.

Derek's teachers
and school friends
wrote letters and poems,
then gave them to us in a book.

A friend asked me
to break her colt –
that filly still fills
a corner of the void.

A man who had
also lost a son
reached out and touched
Bill's shoulder as if to say,
"I know it's hard, but you'll make it."

Each is remembered:

A student from Somalia,
studying at the university,
scaled these peaks of grief
eight times in his few years.
He and his mother faced the death
of his seven brothers and his father.
He called us – at least – twice a month
to see how we were doing and to let us know
he was keeping us in his prayers to Allah.

Those "listeners" had the strength
and secure inner space
to hear and support us
on our painful
and confusing
healing journey.

A Quechua family
we visited
in the Andes of Peru
sent us
a tiny braided cross.

Gifts to Dawna –
a cuddly bunny,
a soft doll
to carry,
to hold.

A young couple
gently reminded us
of Kahlil Gibran's
wise thoughts on parenting:
    Children are not yours.
      Parents are bows from
        which arrows are sent.

The food brought
on disposable plates,
as well as
the food that came in dishes
with the sender's name
marked on the bottom and
which needed to be returned –
a visit that got me out of the house.

Those calls,
the thought-filled notes
on the anniversary
of Derek's death,
on his birthday
to let us know
years later,
others still
remember him.

Loving
blessings
seen, felt
in pain-filled and
peaceful, caring smiles.

The waitress
who, in her pain,
called me Derek.
I thanked her.

Those who
in silence
stood beside us
or held us as we cried
in those anguished
unexpected
awkward moments.

"It feels so good to know you
remember."

The memorial donations
to WORLD NEIGHBORS
continue Derek's efforts
toward food, health,
and dignity for those
less fortunate.

Now, years after his death
his classmates include him
in memory, as a member
on their class T-shirt.

Patient friends
encouraged me to write,
helped edit this manuscript.

He's remembered.

Another mother
just last week
said she missed Derek.
She hugged me;
tears were
in her eyes.

The lights
each year
since his death
on the Hospice Tree –
gifts that not only help
but glimmer in his memory.

Can you imagine what it means
to have someone else say his name?
or say, years later –
"Get the Kleenex out,
I need to talk about Derek."

Each reached out,
each shared,
each helped bear the pain.

Each thought,
  each prayer
    is important –
      far more
        than you think.

It helped our family
when someone

listened

or said,
"I care."
"I'm so sorry."
"I'm hurting too."
"My thoughts are with you."
"I've been thinking about you."
"I need to tell you I miss him."
"I've never told you,
  but I remember Derek doing…"

How could two grief experiences
in one family be so different?

Not even one card
when our first son,
Dylan died –
an incomprehensible contrast.

Thank you
for sitting next to us
and for walking with us
on this, our second climb across
the mountain range of grief.

Ideas for helping others . . .

My Notebook of
HELPFUL REFERENCES

This appendix includes checklists and other helpful information, which was compiled for my own family use out of our experience. These lists have been invaluable to our family and have assisted others as they have faced the need to make pro-active decisions relating to a death.

Being Supportive of Someone Seriously Ill or Injured

Increasingly, it seems, I hear about a friend who is seriously ill. My own serious injury taught me about being supportive without being invasive. (I *have used my friend Beth's name to make these notes read more easily. If the need arises, please substitute the name of your friend or relative to make this your own list.*) Much of this section applies to supporting spouses, partners, children and parents.

It is a shock when I learn that a relative, close friend or someone I know is ill or seriously injured. I'm usually at a loss for words and actions. Illness or injury forces me to look at the fragility of my own life and ask, "Am I doing what is really important?" It is valuable for me to recall we are all in the living and dying process. We may have a warning that our time could be shortened by an illness.

These notes help me move to a place of personal peace so I can express my concern and be a more helpful family member or friend to *Beth* and to *Beth's* family system as we grow through this challenge of incapacity. I want *Beth* to feel and know she is loved, appreciated and thought of in our happy and growing experiences together as friends.

GENERAL — I *want to remember*:

❑ Don't avoid *Beth*, especially now when she needs supportive friends.

❑ Every person's illness or injury is different.

❑ Be the same. Don't markedly change behaviors or routines. Keeping a routine (as much as possible) is comforting. If necessary, substitute activities.

❑ **Listen** and act with intuition, heart and ears. Let *Beth* lead me and others who are with us through this time. Don't smother her.

❑ **Listen** and talk with her about what she is experiencing, the prognosis, treatment. Discussing ~ not ignoring ~ the illness or injury *by name, unless requested otherwise,* will likely help both of us avoid denial and see this as a growth process.

❑ It may be important to remind myself that pain can almost always be managed by additional levels of medication so that a patient is not in discomfort. I may want to ~ or need to ~ be **very** insistent on this point.

❑ Stay flexible and change with *Beth*. Illness or injury changes people and often how they see life. I must accept her changes. If we played tennis, we may need to substitute with a walk or a drive. Her conversation interests may change.

❑ *Beth's* cultural heritage, religious beliefs and family system may be different from my own. Expressing interest and being supportive of her within her belief system can be very helpful to her and build our friendship.

❑ It may be valuable to casually discuss life as being a terminal experience for everyone. I have noticed that those who most often appear to die in peace have usually not put off acting on their dreams of what they want to do in life. I can encourage *Beth* to share her dreams and do what I can to facilitate them.

❑ Be supportive of *Beth's* independence. Respect her wishes and ideas. She needs to do what she wants to do. If I do more for her than is needed, I may want to consider whether I am being loving or controlling. She will likely explore setting and holding new emotional boundaries. This type of assertive change is sometimes harder for family members to accept than it is for friends.

❑ Don't try to talk *Beth* out of emotions she expresses ~ especially ones that are uncomfortable to hear. She needs to have those feelings heard.

PREPARATION – I *want to remember*:

❑ Take at least 30 minutes of quiet time, alone, to gather myself and my thoughts before going to see *Beth* or calling her directly. If Beth tells me of the illness or injury personally, responding "*Oh no!*" is better than "*I'm sorry*" because you are likely not responsible for Beth's condition. A short, honest statement is usually appropriate. (This is also true when talking with a spouse or partner.)

When I *learn of the illness or injury*:

- I've heard you are ill, *Beth*. I don't know what to say. Are you comfortable sharing with me what's going on with your health?

- You are in my thoughts and prayers. I hope you will let me drop by to see you or call you.

- I am here for you. Where can I write my phone number so you can keep it near you? Call me anytime of day or night (*if this is true*) if you need help or want to talk. *Occasionally ask, "Do you still have my phone number handy?"*

- I want to be helpful to you. *Practical help may or may not be needed or appreciated now; this may change later (shopping, food preparation, household chores, child care, watering plants). It is appropriate to ask if she would like a helping hand.*

  Be specific: "*Could I bring dinner over one night this week? Which night is best?*"
       "*Is there anything that you are hungry for or that you prefer not to eat?*"
       "*Can I pick up the children today?*"
       "*Would it help if I watered this plant? How about the others?*"
       "*Thank you for letting me help you.*"

PERSPECTIVE – I *want to remember*:

❑ I will do what I am able to do, within my own obligations, to make sure *Beth* feels cared for and supported (*without adding undue stress in my own life*).

❑ Go to be with *Beth* without any expectations but with the sense of an adventure becoming a growth experience.

❑ Stay present in the moment so I can really be with *Beth* (*not running off in my mind to my fears of the future or slipping into the past*).

❑ Panic and terror likely will need to be expressed by Beth and her family members. It is a rare friend who can open the door and let a person talk deeply about feelings and their injury or illness (*e.g., cancer - it is usually helpful to name the illness*). Be patient. Remember, this is a difficult, emotion-filled time.

❑ To take care of myself, find my own outlets (*counselor, minister, increased exercise and quiet time*) to deal with all of my feelings regarding Beth's illness or injury. The more I take care of my needs, the more present I will be for Beth.

DOING – I *want to remember*:

❑ Be honest and open with my own fears, which may help Beth express her feelings of fear and anger.

❑ Phrases that I have found open the door and seem to be received as supportive *after several visits*:

- "This illness scares me, Beth. Are you scared?"

- "I'm on my way to the store (*or to town*). May I pick up some things for you?"

- "What are some of the things that I could do to help you?"

- "May I help you start a list of how others can help you so when people ask that same question, you don't have to think. You can just look at the list. Let's also include notes about any strong dislikes of food. Do you have smoke, food, allergies, etc.?" (*Post this list near the phone at her bed or at sitting eye level – also inconspicuously by the door.*)

- "Would it be all right if I checked with others (*in our group or church*) to see if they might like to participate in a (child relief or an evening meal in a foil pan,* etc.) rotation until you are feeling better?" (**foil pans because regular dishes take energy to return*)

- "I often think of you when I run across information related to your condition. Could I send or bring that information to you or would you prefer I keep it in a folder?"

❑ **Be sure** to call and drop by for **brief** visits at home or at the hospital. A quick 5-10 minutes can brighten Beth's day. I find it better to vary the timing and spacing of visits so I'm not "expected." This keeps my days more flexible, decreases my guilt and avoids disappointment or resentment if I don't get by or call for several days. (*If I have time, I can ask for an assignment of a chore, do it quickly, then quietly say good-bye and leave. Lingering visitors can be an energy drain.*)

❑ Take time to be with Beth in silence. Solitude is often healing. Let her talk while I visualize her surrounded with healing light as she expresses or even if she holds her thoughts and concerns. Ask her if you can stay a while, to support her in silence.

❑ Hug or hold Beth. (**Be sure to ask first** *if she would like a hug.*) She may want to cry while she is in my arms. (*I want to encourage her to cry if this seems appropriate.*) Physical contact is often helpful and comforting.

❑ Without appearing to be obvious, try breathing with Beth (*don't strain my own body*). Often a precious closeness comes as a result.

❑ Offer to take *Beth* to her doctor, to treatments, for a drive, or to go out to lunch when she feels like doing so.

❑ Ask if she would like me to pick up books, audio tapes or videos from the library.

❑ If she is on medication, do not wear perfume or cologne.

❑ Encourage the taking of a family photograph (*as soon as possible, is a good idea*). Also, *keeping a camera handy during an illness often records very touching and memorable moments.* Working on a memory book, family photo folio and notebook can be a fun project.

❑ Keep blank or "Just thinking of you" cards on hand. Send a card as I think of *Beth* or a clipping about anything I see of interest to *her* with a note written in the margin: "*You crossed my mind when I saw this.*" [*My mother uses old postcards – sending one to say "Hi" and mentioning how it reminds her of the friend (chance to get them reminiscing) when she thinks of the person.*] Mail from a friend is a welcome treat when someone is ill.

❑ A basket of fruit, small portions of healthy snacks or a light, funny or positive book are nice gifts. Sharing photos of mutual friends and recalling memories, a flower from my yard, an interesting stone, or a pine cone that catches my eye shows "I'm thinking of you." (*Thoughtful playfulness is often surprisingly encouraging.*)

❑ The illness of my friend or relative may be a reminder for me to see my attorney to review (*or draw*) my Will, Durable Power of Attorney for Health Care, Living Will and A Letter to My Physician (*see pages* 24-25) or any upon-death instructions. Doing my own homework (*with my attorney, reviewing and filling out pages* 19-25) will allow me to talk about these issues relating to my own experience, rather than asking *Beth* if she has dealt with these documents.

❑ Two or three local friends can work out a schedule to take freshly squeezed orange juice in a small pitcher. It's a precious message and demonstration of caring. Place it on the porch with *Beth's* newspaper on a regular basis, so that it is there when she goes to get her newspaper, rather than disturb her rest.

❑ If you are knowledgeable about insurance forms and filing insurance claims, an offer to responsibly handle this concern area for an ill friend may be most welcome.

SPECIAL THINGS – I *want to remember*:

☆ When I have done what I can do within the constraints of my other obligations, it is important not to flog myself with guilt for not being "the perfect supportive friend or relative." Take a minute to appreciate what I *have done* – no matter how small or large. It all helps.

☆ Other family members and close friends will likely need and appreciate support. They may welcome an invitation for a "cup of coffee or a soda."

☆ Counseling, an Anticipatory Grief Class or hospice training offered by many hospices may be helpful to both friends and family members.

➤➤☆ Children need considerable additional support, reassurance and consistency as they cope with the changes when an important person in their own life is ill. Encourage keeping them abreast of changes and answer their questions honestly in a confirming, comforting way. Taking the child to a movie or park (swinging often has a calming effect), going for walks or picnicking nearby give private time to family members and build a bond that might be helpful later.

☆ *After checking to see if the information is interesting and appropriate*, ask Beth if she would like me to help her research by using the library or the Internet for anticipatory grief information or for details about her illness.

☆ The well-meaning advice given by others to someone ill or injured may need to be filtered through "a thought strainer." Such as "this advice is intended as a gift from someone who is really giving it out of their own fear, to themselves rather than me and/or they cannot tolerate seeing someone disabled, in pain, or ill."

☆ A social worker at the hospital can provide a list of local support agencies (*contact person, phone number and address*, such as Meals on Wheels, support groups, home health care, etc.). You might ask if someone would contact a longtime survivor of Beth's illness who could contact Beth. Someone who has lived with an experience usually has a valued and welcome perspective.

Things I want to remember . . .

Comforting Someone Possibly Near Death

Occasionally life gives us the privilege of being with a person when he or she may be in the last hours of life. (*For the reader's ease in reviewing this list, I have used my Uncle Howard's name. Please substitute your friend's or relative's name to make this **your** own list.*) Like many readers of this book, my middle-class North American upbringing did not prepare me well for these death experiences. Many other cultures give people the supportive tool of tradition around a death.

This list helps me move to a place of peace within myself so I am able to be "present" for the person who is likely near death. I want to free myself from fears and other concerns, to be available, supportive and helpful.

PREPARATION – I *want to remember*:

❑ Take at least 30 minutes of quiet time, alone, to gather myself and my thoughts before going to be with Howard.

❑ I want to do what I am able to do to make sure Howard does not die alone.

❑ Go to be with Howard. Take no expectations but the sense of an adventure growing into a privileged experience.

❑ Know that every death is different.

❑ Listen with my intuition, my heart and my ears. Throughout this time, allow Howard to lead me and others who are with us.

❑ Silence is a precious time to visualize Howard resting in a lovely garden, by a river or in some other peace-filled place.

❑ Play soft, soothing music of a type Howard enjoys.

❑ Be aware of any of Howard's cultural traditions around dying that may be different from my own.

❑ Be aware of these three tasks usually faced at death: (*Hopefully, they have already been dealt with, yet an issue in these areas sometimes arises.*)

1. Legal matters dealt with and **in writing**, including a Will, Durable Power of Attorney for Health Care, A Living Will and A Letter to My Doctor or any upon-death instructions to the family (*see pages 297-309*).

2. Resolution of emotional work left unfinished.

3. Spiritual work that takes the person to a place of inner peace.

DOING – I *want to remember*:

❏ Breathe with the dying person, without straining my own body; often a precious closeness comes as a result.

❏ It may be important to remind myself that pain, especially now, can almost always be managed by additional levels of medication so that a patient is not in discomfort. I may want – to or need to – be insistent on this point.

❏ Think of small acts, which are often desired, for Howard's comfort. The need for these may be communicated in verbal or nonverbal ways.
  • Touching or stroking *his* brow with or without a cool cloth
  • Turning Howard a bit
  • Placing ice chips on lips and moistening lips lightly with lip lubricant
  • Putting a pillow under the knees
  • Hugging or holding Howard in *my* arms (*may be welcomed*)
  • (*When desired*,) lying next to your loved one (*is commonly very comforting to both people*)
  • Reading favored or underlined passages from one of his loved books

❏ Talk with or speak softly to Howard. This may be comforting to both of us; these releasing phrases are often comforting (*if they are appropriate and can be said honestly*):
  • I know you love me (*or us*).
  • I love you.
  • I release you.
  • I forgive you.
  • I surround you with love (*light, beautiful memories, prayer, etc.*) as I release you.
  • I am walking with you in this experience.
  • This is a privilege to be with you now.
  • I want to let you know that it is okay for you to "go" now and that I love you.

SPECIAL THINGS – I *want to remember*:

☆ Take care of myself, eat balanced meals regularly (*even if I am not hungry*) and discipline myself to take frequent rest breaks.

☆ If Howard happens to die while I am out of the room, I want to remember that this is all right. There is much about the timing of death that remains unknown. I can know that I was with him in spirit, in my thoughts (*and/or prayers*). I do know I can be a great distance away and still be holding someone in my thoughts, and be and feel very close to that person.

When Someone Dies: My Checklists

In reading and referring to this list, recall that it was developed for my family in a rural community where I lived much of my life. We lived in a city when our first son died during birth. At that time we did only a few of the things on this list. I have never experienced a death where all items on this list were completed. Every situation is different. This list is only a **general guideline of suggestions**, each of which may or may not be appropriate. Religious, cultural, family system and geographic variations will alter needs. Funeral directors can be asked to handle much of this process; however, there may be additional charges for each item in which they are involved.

Even though arrangements are necessary, it is **vital** that *family members* **not** *feel pressured into making rushed decisions. In addition, we have found it is valuable to take a few moments upon the death, or hearing of the death, and as family and friends gather, to appreciate the blessings and/or lessons this person brought into our lives. The way this appreciation is done will vary by individuals involved and by cultural or religious tradition.*

❤ = Immediate family
✳ = Friends or more distant relatives
◆ = A common point of funeral director participation; there may be charges for each involvement
➤ = Of particular importance when children are involved

> **Note:** *Ideally each child and adolescent in the family should have a consistent, caring, aware adult who is removed enough to be emotionally supportive, observant and able to listen to the young person express feelings and fears in the days before and immediately after a death, and during subsequent weeks and months.*

DAY ONE

❤ 1. If death occurred by accident or in a hospital, make organ donation or medical research decisions, if appropriate. Many families have found considerable solace in a donation decision. *Here, time is usually of the essence.*

❤ 2. Sign hospital papers and releases, if requested.

❤ 3. If death occurred at home, call the doctor, hospice worker, or case nurse to certify death. *Be aware that if* **911** *is called, the Emergency Medical Technicians (EMTs)* **are required by law** *to do everything possible to attempt to resuscitate the dead person unless there is* **A Living Will** *on the premises to show them, or the person is wearing a particular* "DO NOT RESUSCITATE" *bracelet or necklace obtained by a physician's order (in most jurisdictions).* ◆

❤ 4. Follow the directives of the doctor, hospice worker, or case nurse.

✴ 5. Consider taking a copy of this book to the family. Show them this section and perhaps insert a bookmark at page 222.

➡ ❤ 6. Saying good-bye immediately before and after a death, if at all possible, can be very helpful. Everyone who can, and wishes to, should spend as much time as they wish with the deceased. The adequate amount of time cannot be judged for one person by another. Wide variations in the need to see, touch or hold the deceased should be allowed. If additional time is needed, it can be done at the funeral home. Each person should do **only** what **he or she wants to do.** If allowed to be, children are clear on their own needs.

❤ 7. Taking the opportunity to bathe, powder or lotion the body of the deceased is sometimes a tenderly loving and memorable experience for some people. **You will know** if this is something that **you** want to do.

❤ 8. Seeing the body, even after trauma, usually helps survivors with reality of the death and lessens denial. This can usually be done immediately or at any point until disposition. You may wish to consider having a professional counselor present, which can be very helpful for assessment and later help. ♦

➡ ❤ 9. In infant death, in stillbirth, and often even in miscarriage, it is now usually considered advisable to name, hold, dress, photograph and footprint the child. This validates and actualizes the baby's life and is very helpful to grieving parents. Hospital staff will usually be helpful with burial arrangements, along with providing information and follow-up support which are very important, as with any death. *See pages 262, 263 and 274 forinfant memorial cards and service ideas.*

❤ 10. Authorize or decline autopsy unless one is required due to circumstances.

➡ ❤ 11. Notify all immediate family members, including children, of the death. Use the word "died" rather than "went away." (*See page 246 for* NOTES ON CHILDREN AND DEATH.)

❤ 12. When notifying immediate family who will be flying commercially, remind them to ask for an Immediate Family Bereavement Discount offered by many airlines.

❤ 13. Call clergy; often this will be comforting for some or all members of the family. ♦

❤ 14. Assuming an attorney drew the will, locate the attorney holding the current will. (*Hopefully a will exists.*)

❤ 15. Ask attorney if the will contains burial or – upon death – instructions.
   (*It is very important that copies of this information and list of bank Safe Deposit Box contents be kept elsewhere for easy known access, immediately, at the time of need. Remember, the bank Safe Deposit Box is sealed as soon as the bank reads of the death or is notified.*)

♦ Funeral Director   ➡ Children or Youth

❤ 16. Ask the attorney for the name of the executor. (*This is important.*)

❤ 17. Decide upon a funeral home. (*See page* 250, *items* 1-4.)

❤ 18. Give funeral director the location of the deceased and a contact's phone number. This is often done by the hospital unless the family has a preference.

❤ 19. A funeral director will help with out-of-area deaths as they require additional arrangements and transport of the deceased to the service location. ◆

❤ 20. Make an appointment to meet with the funeral director after all persons involved in decision-making have reviewed *items* 25-41 *on pages* 226-229. Allow several hours for your "kitchen table" family discussion. Also, ask if you can pick up a price list of funeral home services.

➥❤ 21. All family members may find it helpful to give thought and discussion time to their expectations and feelings regarding burial traditions, including what they feel were the deceased's wishes. Children's and grandchildren's concerns need to be heard, discussed with them and considered.

➥❤ 22. Arrange for the family meeting. If all immediate family members are not available, a conference call may be a solution. If this is not possible at home, a borrowed office with several phones and a conference room or church facility may be a location to consider for this meeting.

➥❤ 23. A "family kitchen table" review of the decision details and QUESTIONS TO ASK OUR FUNERAL DIRECTOR (*see page* 250) is advisable before meeting with the funeral home representative and making decisions.

    We have learned this is very important for a positive family experience and can avoid problems later. Every effort should be made to have as many family members present as possible. However, due to family dynamics you may need to consider having only siblings and parents in attendance. It is important that all immediate family members feel they have been heard and their views understood and considered.

➥❤ 24. Ask someone in the family to be a facilitator who is sensitive to the need for everyone to have a chance to talk, yet can be firm and not allow anyone to monopolize or interrupt. Non-family facilitators are usually not necessary. Call your local hospice for the names of facilitators in case no one in the family can or will facilitate. Before meeting, a facilitator will find it helpful to review *items* 25-41 *on pages* 226-229 *and the referenced sections.*

    ❤ Immediate Family   ✳ Friends or Relatives

FAMILY MEETING FORMAT IDEAS
(We *have found these guidelines work well for our family.*)

Supplies: Set up table and chairs or chairs in a circle if the group is large (*a lap-held writing surface will be needed*). Have paper and pencil for each person (*this allows notation of ideas and minimizes the temptation to interrupt*). Put a small "passable" stone or object on the table. Have boxes of tissues available. Have a copy of this book for the facilitator to use during the meeting.

Facilitator: As a group, agree on the facilitator.

Recorder: It is important to have a participant take notes on all decisions. The Recorder then reads back each decision for agreed approval by the group before going on to the next item of discussion. Copies of the decisions need to be available to participants. Each member of the "family representative team" (*decided in this meeting*) who will meet with the funeral director will likely want a copy of the decisions made at this meeting.

Time: Because time is of essence, it is important to share as briefly as possible so that all necessary items can be decided. Agree on an appropriate (*two to five minutes*) maximum time for comment on each item by each participant. Voting with a thumbs up (*agree*) or thumbs down (*disagree*) often speeds the process.

Center and come together as a group: The facilitator may want to acknowledge the difficulty and strain people are experiencing. It is advisable to mention the deceased's name and state that the reason for the meeting is to find solutions that work for the majority of the family and to make the necessary decisions promptly and together. The goal is that the next few days be as cohesive a family or group experience as possible. Acknowledge that there will likely be strong and differing ideas expressed, especially if the deceased did not leave clear and written instructions. Explain that the stone (*or small object*) will be passed among participants as they share their ideas during the meeting. Ask the group: "Can we focus our attention on the stone for a moment? It will help us keep our minds and thoughts in this room. We need to leave the rest of our day and life outside this room. This will be helpful in order to come up quickly with workable solutions to the 16 decisions we need to review and resolve consensus."

The stone (or object) should be explained: Using a stone is a way to remember that no one is to talk unless he or she is holding the stone. No one interrupts *the stone-holding* speaker except the facilitator. This would be done only if the person begins to monopolize the meeting by talking more than an agreed upon number of minutes. The stone will go from hand to hand until everyone has expressed themselves on the issue or says "I pass." It then goes around the second time for additional thoughts. The decision is called for, recorded, read back and approved. Approval is an important step and should not be overlooked.

Close the meeting after discussing items 25-41 on pages 226-229 on this list. We have found it is important to end the meeting with each person sharing at least a one-sentence appreciation to someone in the group or about this meeting experience.

◆ Funeral Director   ➥ Children or Youth

❤ 25. Review deceased's "Burial and Funeral Instructions" (*see pages* 298-305 *for sample* LETTER OF INSTRUCTION).

❤ 26. Is burial or cremation the preference of the decedent or (*if no instructions*) the preference of a majority of the family?

❤ 27. Decide whether you want a funeral, memorial service, additional services or no service at all.

> **Note:** A *service of some type is far more important than people anticipate. The service will help survivors with reality, recollection, expression and support.*

❤ 28. It is helpful to read over the MEMORIAL OR FUNERAL SERVICE DETAILS section (*pages 269-272*) aloud together **before starting** the discussion of plans for the service.

❤ 29. Allow adequate time (*usually four to seven days after the death*) when deciding the time and place of the service.

> **Points to consider in this decision:**
>
> ❏ time to notify friends and family,
>
> ❏ travel time to the service site,
>
> ❏ obituary notices may take several days for publication; make sure there is at least two full days between publication and the day of the service,
>
> ➨ ❏ time of service should be set after school if many young people are likely to be involved,
>
> ❏ an 11:00 a.m. service allows more working people to attend on weekdays,
>
> ❏ a Friday or weekend service may help those who must travel from out of town,
>
> ❏ time to design, prepare and print a personalized memorial card, if desired (*see page 256*),
>
> ❏ if the service is to be scheduled at a church, choose one of appropriate size and denomination. Times of availability may be a consideration in choosing locations,
>
> ❏ if not a church, the funeral home chapel or the choice of a meaningful location that is easy to find are other alternatives,
>
> ❏ if a fraternal order will be involved in the service, request their assistance promptly.

❤ 30. The time and place of services **must** be confirmed after you meet with the funeral director and before most notifications, to avoid unnecessary calls.

❤ 31. Whom do you want to officiate at the service: clergy and/or family and friends? Participatory services are especially helpful in the grieving process and can be very meaningful experiences.

❤ 32. Does the family prefer flowers or contributions, in lieu of flowers, to a charitable memorial, educational or research fund?

❤ 33. Review PREPARING A PERSONALIZED MEMORIAL CARD and the sample card information (*see pages* 256-266).

❤ 34. Decide if a personalized memorial card is important to the family.

❤ 35. Decide who can and will design the personalized memorial card and what might be included on it. This can be a very healing project for a family member or friend who has computer skills.

❤ 36. Decide who will collect the information and write the obituary (*see list on page* 228). ♦

❤ 37. Decide which two or three family members will meet as the "family representative team" with the funeral director. Be sure to have at least one number-detail-oriented person at these meetings and confirm that each team member has carefully reviewed costs (*item* 41 *on page* 229).

❤ 38. Discuss the family need for assistance with child care or the care of older family members for the next several days. Keep the family together as much as possible, yet honor individual space needs. Assistance in these concerns can markedly reduce stress. Friends can be helpful resources.

❤ 39. Set the time and place for the family to meet again for a second "kitchen table" discussion to review the funeral director's suggestions, to make decisions on the service and firm up other details. It is also important to see the memorial card ideas on paper.

♦ Funeral Director   ➤ Children or Youth

❤ 40. Collect the following information, as appropriate. All or some of it will be required for burial permit, obituary notice, and in closing details of the death.

- full, legal name
- nickname
- religious name
- city and state of residence
- how long in state
- age
- date of birth
- place of birth
- country of citizenship
- spouse's name
- maiden name
- father's name
- father's birthplace
- mother's maiden name
- mother's birthplace
- religious affiliation
- occupation and title
- type of business
- business address and phone
- social security number
- veteran's serial number
- cause of death
  (*if service was before* 1972)

- place of death
- memberships
- grade schools
- high schools attended
- colleges attended
- degrees
- scholarships
- positions held in public service or in religious affiliations
- awards, honors, meritorious citations
- military service
- date of enlistment
- date of discharge
- military honors
- list of surviving immediate family members
- hobbies and special interests
- special accomplishments
- famous family members
- special wishes or charitable donations

Additional Information: _____

_____

_____

_____

_____

_____

Obituary notice: *If you wish to write this notice, you will need to add only the time and location of the service to this list after you have met with the funeral director. Many families find value in writing the obituary; check with the newspaper for requirements and* costs. *The funeral director will provide this service, usually at a charge, if asked to do so.*

❤ Immediate Family   ✳ Friends or Relatives

❦41. The cost range our family can afford to consider is:

Cost   **Minimum**   **$** _____   **– Maximum**   **$** _____

↘ Record initials of person who has agreed to be responsible for this detail.

$ _____   _____   ❏ chapel use

_____   _____   ❏ personalized memorial cards

_____   _____   ❏ memorial service

_____   _____   ❏ funeral

_____   _____   ❏ graveside service, interment/Public? Private? Clergy?

_____   _____   ❏ casket or urn (*listed prices range up to $25,000, our range* ($ – $)

         (_funeral home pruchase, _homemade [*see page 275*], _construct pre-cut kit)

_____   _____   ❏ vault

_____   _____   ❏ cemetery plot location

_____   _____   ❏ headstone or marker

_____   _____   ❏ endowment care of cemetery plot

_____   _____   ❏ opening and closing of the grave

_____   _____   ❏ floral arrangements

         _____   ❏ memorial donations in lieu of flowers

_____   _____   ❏ funeral coach

_____   _____   ❏ limousines for family members

_____   _____   ❏ limousines for pallbearers

_____   _____   ❏ vehicle for transporting flowers

         _____   ❏ pallbearers

_____   _____   ❏ cremation

_____   _____   ❏ embalming and preparation

_____   _____   ❏ restorative art

_____   _____   ❏ makeup

_____   _____   ❏ hair (*asking for a lock of hair is not unreasonable*)

_____   _____   ❏ nails

_____   _____   ❏ glasses

_____   _____   ❏ jewelry (*you may choose to have rings removed just prior to burial*)

_____   _____   ❏ religious or fraternal items

_____   _____   ❏ clothing for the deceased

_____   _____   ❏ viewing the deceased

_____   _____   ❏ open casket service

_____   _____   ❏ visitation hours for family (*cost/hour or visit*)

_____   _____   ❏ visitation hours for others (*cost/hour or visit*)

_____   _____   ❏ clothing for the family
         (*purchase suits, slacks, or dresses for family members, if needed*)

_____   _____   ❏ haircuts and hair appointments for family members

_____   _____   ❏ music   ❏ taped   ❏ live   ❏ both

_____   _____   ❏ organist/pianist   ❏ other _____ (e.g. guitar)

_____   _____   ❏ soloist

_____   _____   ❏ audio or video recording of service

_____   _____   ❏ memorial record book with guest register

_____   _____   ❏ photographs of family and deceased for photo display

_____   _____   ❏ acknowledgment cards

_____   _____   ❏ parking facilities

_____   _____   ❏ police escort and traffic control

_____   _____   ❏ signing necessary papers

_____   _____   ❏ obituary notices

_____   _____   ❏ death certificates # _____ needed

_____   _____   ❏ officiating person(s)

$ _____   **Review total cost of each item and total** *against budget guidelines* **before** *making final decisions and signing funeral home agreements.*

❤   42.   Call **a few close, helpful** family friends. Call memorial organization for overnight delivery of envelopes for display at the service or after service gathering (*attendees will appreciate your thoughtfulness for their convenience.*) Most of the other informing calls can be made by family and friends later.

❤   43.   Ask close friends and family to be available to answer the phone and greet visitors. An answering machine or e-mail with a frequently updated message may be a solution, yet it will lack the personal contact of a caring friend. A friend or family member can answer questions, hear concerns, take messages and eliminate many time-consuming call-backs.

❤   44.   Near the phone, keep the number of an available doctor in case someone needs medical assistance.

✱❤   45.   Start lists of the following information: (*each list in a separate spiral notebook or on clipboard, return* (✱) *list to one area after using for locating convenience*)
    A. ☐ all pertinent facts for callers (*include service and memorial information*)
    B. ☐ all PHONE CALLS (*keep lists A and B next to each phone*)
    C. ☐ all GIFTS – get name and address
    D. ☐ all FOOD – get name and address
    E. ☐ anyone who OFFERS TO HELP (*get phone number, name and address, and what he or she has offered to do*)

❤   46.   Make a list or copy the deceased's address book for notification of immediate family, close friends and business associates. Color coding can be helpful. (*See items 75 -78 on page 234 in this list, for notifying others. Most of these calls can be made later.*)

✱❤   47.   Immediate family and close friends should check their calendars. Consider cancelling appointments coming up within the next few days.

✱   48.   Check calendar of the deceased and notify those individuals scheduled on it. Calls are often more easily made by a friend.

✱❤   49.   Start an "Our Memories of _____" notebook. A loose-leaf binder works well. First pages are List of Visitors and Helpers. Friends and family can add pages of pictures (*note names and dates*), drawings and written pieces. Place the binder - along with extra pages - on the coffee table; encourage people to participate in the project.

✱❤   50.   Start a WHAT CAN BE DONE LIST as needs occur to you - things that might be helpful or could be done when callers ask if they can do anything. People like to be given jobs to do during this time, such as play with or watch children, visit or sit with older family members, go to the store, weed the yard, vacuum, repair (*the porch, the faucet, etc.*), wash windows, dust, do laundry, do chores, feed animals, walk pets, mow the lawn, etc. (*see pages* 277-280). Keep this list by the phone.

❤ Immediate Family   ✱ Friends or Relatives

WHAT CAN BE DONE LIST

Note: *Who has offered to do it?*   *Name, Address and Phone Number*

LISTEN with your quiet, supportive presence
Visit the family
Take copy of this book to the family
Answer the phone
Write out your favorite memories of the deceased
Make phone calls
Bring dinner
Bring toilet paper, vitamins and tissues
Help with the memorial card
Arrange for videotaping the service
Take family members to the funeral home
Find someone responsible and uninvolved to housesit during the funeral
Look among your photographs for meaningful pictures
Help make a picture board and/or display of meaningful objects (*for the service entrance
     area or after-service gathering or both, include memorial envelopes for attendees' convenience*).
Start a coffee table "Visitors /Memory Book"
Go to the store, get needed items and any basics, bread, fruit, juices, coffee, tea.
Vacuum
Play with or watch the children
Visit with older family members
Mow the lawn
Help with chores
Attend the guest register
Be a greeter at the service or after-service gathering
Set up for the after-service gathering
Bring food to the after-service gathering
Transport flowers from service to gathering
Help serve and clean up the after-service gathering
     1.
     2.
     3.
     4.
Deliver extra flower arrangements after gathering
Help in returning dishes
Call or visit the family members frequently

See pages 277-283 for additional ideas of things you might offer to do.

Note: *Placing this list horizontally on a page leaves room for recording the name,
address and phone number of anyone who offers to help. This is a nice memory addition
in the folio notebook.*

     ♦ Funeral Director   ➤ Children or Youth

✻ 51. As a friend, you might offer to assist with or arrange child care or the care of older family members for the next several days. It is important to keep the family together as much as possible, yet honor individual space needs.

❤✻ 52. Label all dishes and food containers as they arrive with name and phone number for easy return; get address, if possible (*it will be helpful information in returning dish*).

✻ 53. Visit the decedent's family as soon and as often as possible. **Listen**, don't talk much, encourage sharing memories. Take healthful food and go for a "listening walk" with a family member.

✻ 54. After listening and visiting for a while, ask if you can help by answering the door and taking phone calls. Be aware of other needs. Then offer to be of specific assistance.

➡✻ 55. A soft, cuddly toy is often a thoughtful and comforting gift for both children and adults.

❤✻ 56. Be aware that everyone involved is under stress.

❤✻ 57. Consider taking vitamins, especially for stress.

❤✻ 58. Get outside in the sunshine and fresh air. When friends come to visit, suggest taking a "talking walk" together.

❤✻ 59. Do everything possible to see that survivors and friends eat well-balanced meals. (*Severe loss of appetite often occurs for immediate family members and others close to the deceased.*) SIT DOWN to meals regularly — even if you don't want to eat or are not hungry.

❤✻ 60. If possible, sit down in a quiet place. Reflect on special memories, jot down a few ideas. This may be the beginning of a poem, prose piece or song you might choose to share at the service.

❤✻ 61. Sleep — or at least rest. Very important!

❤✻ 62. If you are having trouble sleeping, write your thoughts out on paper. This may give your mind permission to rest.

❤ Immediate Family   ✻ Friends or Relatives

DAY TWO

✳❤ 63. If you awaken early or are a morning person, the quiet of the morning may be your only time to reflect on special memories and jot your ideas down. Again, these moments of reflection may be the beginning of a poem, prose piece or song you might choose to share at the service. Even if not shared, it gets your thoughts out on paper. It frees your mind and eliminates some stress.

❤ 64. Before the family representative team meets with the funeral director, review QUESTIONS TO ASK OUR FUNERAL DIRECTOR, *page 250*.

❤ 65. Discuss with your funeral director the items on *pages 250-254* that are appropriate to your situation. Also see the preference and cost range information sheet from *page* 229. You will likely find the funeral director is very helpful and has many creative and usable ideas.

❤ 66. Ask about funeral home visitation hours and costs.

❤ 67. If you have any special need or problems, your funeral director has undoubtedly helped others solve the same ones. Ask for suggestions.

➺❤ 68. Your funeral director can help make arrangements for care of children, as well as for ill or elderly immediate family members, during the service. Some funeral homes have children's rooms with a supervisor. ◆

❤ 69. Get three or more copies of the funeral director's written estimate. Allow time to review it with the family privately at a second and finalizing "kitchen table" family discussion.

❤ 70. Before leaving the funeral home, make a second appointment with the funeral director to convey the family decisions to be made at the family meeting. This appointment should be the day following the meeting, if possible, to allow for family discussion time.

❤ 71. Begin designing — or delegate the designing of — the memorial card if you do not wish to use the regular funeral home style. Have the family approve content and layout at the finalization meeting. (*See pages 256-266 for ideas and instructions.*) ◆

❤ 72. If pallbearers are going to be used, six must be selected and notified as soon as possible.

❤ 73. Honorary pallbearers are an option when health or mobility precludes participation due to the lifting involved.

❤ 74. Check with family and close friends coming from out of town to see if they need hotel accommodations or transportation. Ask a friend or other family member to assist with details. ♦

❤ 75. Delegate most of the notification process, if possible. Usually it is easier for others, rather than the immediate family, to make these calls.
   ❑ The funeral director will make notification phone calls and will usually charge for this service.
   ❑ Organizations often have phone committees that will notify local members of a death.
   ❑ An answering machine may be helpful (*especially if there are few people to help*).

❤ 76. Remember that nurses and other caregivers frequently appreciate being notified and invited to services, as a close relationship often evolves in cases of prolonged illness.

❤ 77. When asking others to make the notification phone calls, give them written, brief details of the death, information about the service times and place, and memorial gift details, if requested in lieu of flowers.

✷ 78. Make remaining notification phone calls. ♦

❤ 79. Complete the obituary notices, adding memorial donation information (*if that is the family wish in lieu of flowers*); add a contact name and phone number for additional information. The funeral director may be asked to take care of this detail. ♦

❤ 80. Do not place a home address in the obituary notices. Unfortunately, this can act as an announcement that the home will be vacant during the specified time of the funeral.

❤ 81. Obituary notices can be delivered in person or faxed to the newspapers. Consider including a fairly current photo of the deceased. Some newspapers use obituary photos.

✷ 82. Make sure nutritious food will be provided for the immediate family so that no cooking will be necessary for several days. When people call to inquire about what food they may bring, suggest healthful casseroles, vegetable dishes, salads or fresh fruit rather than sweets and desserts.

❤ 83. Instead of saying "Call me if I can help," offer to do something specific: "Would it help if I came over and helped vacuum or wash windows while the family is at the funeral home?" "I'm handy and have tools; does anything need to be fixed?"

❤ Immediate Family   ✷ Friends or Relatives

❤ 84. Meet again as a family in a finalization "kitchen table" discussion to review the funeral director's suggestions and firm up plans for the services, memorial card, the after-service gathering and any other details.

❤ 85. Begin by reviewing aloud MEMORIAL OR FUNERAL SERVICE DETAILS on *page* 269.

❤ 86. Decide who will facilitate the services; some families prefer to conduct their own with the help of friends. *See pages* 178-200 for an actual example of a participatory service. These services can still include clergy who take a minor rather than a major role.

❤ 87. Decide who will request the assistance of clergy, if desired, for the service.
- ❏ Make appointment.
- ❏ Gather eulogy materials, poems, stories, meaningful Scripture.
- ❏ Favorite books of the deceased are often marked with passages that were especially meaningful and may be helpful in planning the service.
- ❏ Recall favorite songs. The deceased's tape — and record — storage area is a good resource (*listen to all music to be used and review words to avoid surprises*).
- ❏ Meet with clergy and express service preferences.

❤ 88. Plan a comfortable amount of time for service. Forty-five minutes is common (*range is usually from 25 minutes to 2 hours*).

Service can include:

Music	• played as people arrive and exit
Opening	• states the reason for gathering, usually along with prayer, Scripture reading, poem or other material
Singing	• may be solo, choral or attendees
Service	• liturgy, remembrances by family and friends (*experiences — both good and hard times*)
Announcement	• invitation to after-service gathering, including location — or posted maps at door
Closing	• possibly combines songs, Scripture reading, poetry or prayer

❤ 89. Seriously consider videotaping the service and possibly a bit of the after-service gathering (*both are meaning-filled events, with people who may rarely come together*). A videotape is a **very** *helpful grief tool* for some family members and is often important to those unable to attend or who come into the family later. A professional or an experienced friend can do this nearly unnoticed, especially if a tripod is used.♦

> **Note:** *Participatory memorial services are* **especially meaningful to have videotaped.** *Professionally filmed videos are usually edited. They are very worthwhile and may not necessarily be expensive.*

♦ Funeral Director　　　➥ Children or Youth

❤ 90. After-service gatherings are extremely important. They allow friends and family to be together in a relaxed atmosphere.

> **Remember:** *Friends want to help in any way they can. A potluck-style gathering is usually the easiest solution and provides a way for friends to assist. This also provides the grieving family with food for several days and some to be frozen for use later.*

✳❤ 91. Buffet-style food service and finger food are advisable.
- ❑ Pizza delivered is especially appropriate if the deceased was a young person and many young people are involved.
- ❑ Serve hors d'oeuvres and sandwiches or even just dessert.
- ❑ Caterers are helpful and make it very neat and easy but are, of course, more expensive than a potluck.

✳❤ 92. Decisions about the after-service gathering need to be made: location, menu and who will help.

✳ 93. Accept after-service gathering responsibility and coordinate details and cleanup. It is tremendously helpful if a friend of a friend who does not go to the service is involved in coordinating and helping organize this gathering.

✳ 94. Post at the service exit, a map to the after-service gathering with the reference point of the service location. ◆

✳ 95. Offer to take food to the gathering.

❤ 96. Order altar flowers, casket spray and family floral arrangements to be used during the service. ◆

✳❤ 97. Gather any photos you have of the deceased and share them with the family when you visit or in a note. Be sure to identify people in the picture and put the date on the back. If possible, include a favorite memory about why or when the picture was taken. Put your name and address on the back of the photo *and a notation: Please return, if you wish to have it returned.*

✳❤ 98. A "picture board" or display of memorable items is often a meaningful experience. Ask people to bring and place pictures of the deceased in the funeral home lobby or service entry area. Often people go to a service who have had little recent contact with the family. Pictures are good updating tools when words may be difficult. Memorial donation envelopes can be placed at the edge of the display for family-favored charities. These are appreciated reminders to guests. (*Duplicates of pictures can be made and easily enlarged on a color copy machine.*)

✳ 99. Take responsibility for creating and/or transporting "picture board" or display to gathering after the service.

✳ 100. Make arrangements for a friend's friend to housesit during the funeral to prevent theft. If theft is of high concern, consider using a private security agency. ♦

❤ 101. If the family does not know which music they want performed, clergy or your funeral director will have suggestions. Indicate what music or songs would be unacceptable or offensive to family members. Listen to **all music** and **all words** of **each song**; arrangements often differ. ♦

❤ 102. Select musicians or ask for recommendations from clergy or the funeral director. ♦

❤ 103. Contact musicians and ask about fees. ♦

❤ 104. Specify what music the family wishes to be used. ♦

❤ 105. Hire musicians. ♦

❤ 106. You may prefer to ask the funeral director to coordinate music details after providing your cost and preference guidelines.

❤ 107. Privately review *all* planned and already incurred costs so there are no surprises after the services are over. This is most easily done by reviewing the family preference and cost page (*item* 41 *on page* 229) along with the funeral home estimate.

DAY THREE

❤ 108. The family representative team meets with the funeral director for the second time.

❤ 109. Arrange remaining details for interment or graveside services.
   ☐ private
   ☐ public, immediately after the service
   ☐ clergy and/or only with family

❤ 110. Review *all* planned and already incurred costs and finalize any remaining decisions with the funeral director.

♦ Funeral Director   ➤ Children or Youth

❤111. Carefully review and sign necessary papers at the funeral home.

✷❤112. Relish this time of visiting with friends and relatives. It is a very special time of sharing.

⋯113. Visit the family. Offer to answer the phone, help, etc. (*see page* 277).

⋯114. At the services, a memorial record book with guest register is meaningful for most families. Offer to attend to this detail. ◆

⋯115. Offer to — or arrange to have someone else — take snapshots at the after-service gathering. This is an extended family photo opportunity — a chance to take snapshots in a relaxed, informal setting. (P*ut developed copies in the memory book.*)

✷❤116. Begin preparations for the informal gathering after the service (*extra tables, chairs, table service, etc.*) if it is the following day.

✷117. Offer to help transport flowers after the services if this detail is not arranged through the funeral director. It's nice to have someone take care of the flowers so family members are free to visit with service attendees. (A *family member is often the one who volunteers for this task.*) However, we have found that a friend dealing with the flowers is preferable. It frees family members to relax and take this rare opportunity to visit with relatives and friends.

⋯118. Check to see if the family would appreciate having some of the flower arrangements delivered to hospitals, schools, businesses, or care centers after the services or gathering so they can be further enjoyed by others — then do it. Too many flower arrangements often become overwhelming and depressing when they wilt at home in the days after the services.

⋯119. Make sure to delegate (*habitually prompt*) individuals to be at the service location 30 minutes early to set up and to greet and visit with early-arriving guests, hand out memorial and/or "I remember …" cards (*see page* 265).

⋯120. Delegate a family member or two — not formally participating at the service — to go immediately to the after-service gathering location to greet promptly arriving guests.

⋯121. As people bring food to the gathering, be sure a person is responsible for labeling dishware. This can be done on the bottom of each item with masking tape and a felt-tip pen. Label it with name, phone number and address of giver.

DAY OF THE SERVICE

*122. Continue preparations for the informal gathering after the service, including picking up and straightening the house after family members leave early for the service.

*123. Consider designating after-service gathering greeters. They can have a table with extra guest sheets for the memorial record book by the door for people to sign.

*124. Name tags are sometimes a thoughtful idea for the after-service gathering and can be on the same table as the guests' register.

*125. Consider having folio or notebook sheets titled "My Favorite Memories of_____." These can be on the table with the guests' register sheets. Friends and family members can take a memory page home. Be sure to print the return address at the bottom of each page. These will encourage people to write their recollections. These pages are a precious gift to the family when returned. They can then be placed in the notebook. *See card on page* 260.

*126. Freeze leftovers in meal-size packages (*be sure they are labeled*).

*127. Tidy up kitchen and house after the guests leave.

*128. Vacuum.

♥129. Rehang photos if they were used in photo display at service and gathering. Make duplicates and return borrowed photos.

♥130. Dispose of or rework and water any tired flower arrangements.

♥131. Plan a day of rest and visiting with the family the day after the service. The preceding days will have been very stressful.

WITHIN THREE WEEKS OF THE DEATH

♥132. Notify college and university alumni journals, professional associations, fraternal organizations, religious publications and trade journals. Include photo. ♦

♥133. Remember that many national special-interest magazines and periodicals, such as *Alaska Magazine* and *National Quarter Horse News*, appreciate receiving — and will publish — notifications. ♦

♦ Funeral Director   ➤ Children or Youth

✸❤ 134. Remind and encourage family members to take care of themselves. Grief is hard and stressful emotional work.

❤ 135. Locate and contact local grief support groups (*see page* 311).

   Note: *We have found these groups helpful immediately. They have helped us normalize and balance the changes, feelings and experiences we are having. Other survivors find that six to eight months after a death is a good time for involvement.*

✸ 136. Continue to visit, correspond with, call family members and **listen.**

❤ 137. Make a list of yet-to-be-notified persons who live out of the area. Notify them by card or letter (*include a memorial card*). This can be done in a duplicated holiday letter or note, if not before. (*See examples on pages* 260-261, 265, 291-295.)

❤ 138. Make a list of people to send thank-you notes for flowers, calls, food and other thoughtful gestures.

✸❤ 139. Purchase and help write or address the notes **if help is wanted.** These notes may be printed (*see pages* 260-261 *and on* 265 *the sample was included with a memorial card*) or handwritten. Some families use a less personal notice in the local newspaper or do both — a notice promptly and notes later (*this removes some stress*).

❤ 140. Prepare notice of appreciation for the newspapers or select the publication's standard format.

✸❤ 141. Return dishes (*left after gathering*). This is a nice place to begin with the thank-you note process (*if you wish to do so*).

❤ 142. Obtain six or more Certified Death Certificates, which are needed for official notifications, all securities transfers and other reasons for proof of death.

❤ 143. Notify landlord. Review rental or lease agreements and make any addendum changes. If the person lived alone, terminate agreement and make moving and storage arrangements.

❤ 144. Notify auto/life insurance companies and file request for premium refunds.

❤ 145. Notify and check the following for possible benefits for survivors:
   - ❏ Social Security Administration
   - ❏ Veterans Administration
   - ❏ Retirement fund
   - ❏ Pension fund
   - ❏ Life insurance
   - ❏ Credit unions
   - ❏ Trade unions

❤ 146. Notify and provide name changes:

❑ **Accounts payable** (*Ask for more time before payments are due, if necessary. Check on life or mortgage insurance clauses that may cancel debt upon death.*)

❑ **Correspondents** (*Send cards provided by post office*)

❑ **Bank and credit unions**
- ❑ Savings accounts
- ❑ Safe-deposit boxes
- ❑ Money market accounts
- ❑ Credit card accounts
- ❑ Accounts
- ❑ Checking accounts
- ❑ Trust funds
- ❑ Savings & loans
- ❑ IRAs
- ❑ Loans

❑ **County recorder**
- ❑ Titles and deeds to property

❑ **Certified financial planner**
- ❑ Financial review and necessary changes

❑ **Insurance**
- ❑ Auto
- ❑ Health
- ❑ Personal property
- ❑ Insurance policies owned by others (*should have beneficiary change*)

❑ **Stockbroker**
- ❑ Stocks
- ❑ Bonds
- ❑ Mutual funds

❑ **CPA review tax situation**
- ❑ Federal
- ❑ State
- ❑ Estate
- ❑ Inheritance

❑ **Attorney**
- ❑ Change will's beneficiary (*if deceased was the named beneficiary*)
- ❑ Other will changes

❑ **Vehicle**
- ❑ Vehicle registration
- ❑ Licensing
- ❑ Title
- ❑ Driver's license cancellation

❑ **Utility companies**
- ❑ Telephone listing
- ❑ Billing change – electric, gas, propane, water, TV

❑ **Charge accounts**

❑ **Others who send bills**

❑ **Organizations**
- ❑ Fraternal
- ❑ Civic
- ❑ Social

Other Changes...

♦ Funeral Director   ➥ Children or Youth

❤ 147. Secure home if deceased was living alone. The Police Department, if notified, will often make periodic checks on a home vacated under this circumstance.

❤ 148. Make appointment with attorney for reviewing will and other beneficiary matters.

❤ 149. Pack, move and secure storage for belongings until they can be sorted. Sorting is not usually necessary immediately.

❤ 150. Consider keeping the structure (*or even adding some, if there is very little routine*) in your life. A regular-hours work schedule (*lightened a bit is advisable*). Quitting a job, dropping out of school or out of all activities can complicate the grieving process.

MONTHS AFTER DEATH (*Remember, you have the right to grieve.*)

✳❤ 151. Continue to add to the Guest/Memory Notebook or begin making up a folio memory book of the cards and letters and "My Favorite Memories of _____" sheets, along with photos taken at the gathering and copies of your favorite pictures of the deceased. In many cases this is enjoyable and healing, yet sometimes is a painful project that can be done alone or with a friend or family members.

❤ 152. If at all possible, **DO NOT make long-term decisions** regarding a move, sale of home, investments, large gifts or donations until a year or more after a death.

❤ 153. Get involved and continue attending a local grief support group.

❤ 154. Decide on gravestone and inscription, and order it after seeing and approving a layout printout. This avoids errors. ◆

❤ 155. Check on completion of gravestone or marker. *See* and approve the inscription actually on the marker *before* setting a date for placement.

❤ 156. Two or more months after death, arrange for placement of the marker. This is another good opportunity for a family gathering.

❤ 157. Sorting stored belongings can be done in stages. Clothing is usually sorted first, objects and books next, then memorabilia. "Would _____ want this item to go to someone special?" "Who can use this?" will be helpful questions. Goodwill, Salvation Army and many other local agencies will usually pick up donated items. Libraries usually appreciate donations of books and tapes.

❤ Immediate Family   ✳ Friends or Relatives

💜 158. It may be helpful (*for tax purposes*), to keep a list of all donated items.

✳ 159. Continue to visit, jot notes, call the family and **listen.**

EVERYONE 160. Also, on occasion, especially on the anniversary of the death or birthday of the deceased, call and/or send an *"I've been thinking of you"* card to family members. They will be notified if you make a memorial donation in the deceased's name to a charity.

💜 161. Think in terms of five-minute blocks of time rather than in days or hours of work. Remember these words from *page* 107:

"Five minutes:
dust,
trim a bush,
set the table,
water plants,
make a salad,
wash one window,
clean the bathroom,
straighten the living room,
unload-reload the dishwasher."

💜 162. It is often helpful to write a long or short letter to the deceased that you may wish to keep or burn. You may find it helpful to include your feelings of love, anger, fear, resentment, forgiveness, and appreciation. The same format can be used in writing a letter about your feelings to other surviving family members and friends.

💜 161. One of the most difficult challenges for those who are grieving is learning how to help those who wish to be supportive to be of real assistance to you. Following are a few ideas.
- When someone started to preach to me about what they thought I needed to believe, I found myself responding kindly yet firmly, with "I appreciate your concerns. I am in too much pain to hear what you are saying. Could I ask you to silently hold me/my family in your thoughts and prayers instead?"
- Instead of just saying "Thank you" when someone asks "How can I help you?" you or they can refer to a list, *such as that on page* 277.
- Ask a friend, "Do you have a few minutes to listen? I need to hear his memory, again. It will release the pressure of my pain."
- Please use _____'s name. I need to hear someone else say her/his name" or "Would you tell me a memory of _____ you recall?"

♦ Funeral Director   ➤ Children or Youth

EVERYONE 162. For a reality check, I find it a good idea to occasionally acknowledge a loved one's death out loud to someone else. "_____died _____years ago and I'm missing her right now. This tree reminded me of her. She always told a story about these trees."

EVERYONE 163. It is important for those who have "after death communication" experiences with the deceased (*called* ADC's) to know that these are not uncommon. If this occurrence happens to you, it is **not abnormal** and can be very meaningful. If you have the need, call a counselor or someone with whom you will feel safe discussing the experience.

EVERYONE 164. Make an appointment with a counselor if you are struggling with grief — even years after a death. Many professionals, hospice and other groups offer counseling to individuals and families. This can be very helpful in coming to terms with grief, its anger and associated problems.
(*After seventeen years of quiet, internal grieving for our first son, Dylan, I finally realized I needed counseling and sought help. I had not said good-bye to him because I didn't know a good-bye was as necessary as it is when a baby I never really knew dies. This is as true with a stillborn, a miscarriage or often even after an abortion.*)

EVERYONE 165. **Remember:** It is **NEVER too late** to ask for professional help with grief. If you experience winter depression, you may wish to inquire about "light therapy."

EVERYONE 166. Take care of yourself. **No one else can do it for you.**

I *want to remember to do* ...

❤ Immediate Family   ✷ Friends or Relatives

Children and Serious Illness, Injury or Death in the Family

(Adults would do well to read and follow this list for themselves.)

Support and reassurance for children and teenagers are imperative as a family goes through grief, serious illness or accident recuperation. Children who grieve, or experience a serious illness or injury with a close family member will see life from a different and likely complicating perspective. It is important to provide additional support and compassion for young people.

*(I have used my friend Beth's and my Uncle Howard's names to make these notes read more easily. [Beth and her husband have two boys, 7 and 9, plus nieces and nephews.] Beth's name is used when referring to illness and injury. Uncle Howard's name is used when items relate to a death. [He died peacefully at 94, with his wife, his son, my husband and I at his bedside.] If the need arises, please substitute the name of your friend or relative to make this **your** own list.)*

I am not a therapist. These are notes on the concepts we have learned from family experiences. Every situation differs, yet children will usually lead the way to meeting their needs if others **listen and are observant**.

REMEMBER WITH CHILDREN AND ADOLESCENTS:

1. Communicate with each of them individually and in a supportive way. Use a simple explanation of the death, illness or incapacitating problem. Small bits of information will usually generate questions. These will lead you in your age-appropriate discussion. Overexplaining may be confusing. Possibly use: "Beth's or Uncle Howard's body is not working as well as it used to because Beth *(has cancer or was in an accident - whatever the case)*." In a death, one possibility is "Beth's body stopped working because _____ or *(an accident)*." If a death has occurred, use the word "died" and the decedent's name.

Do not use other explanations with a child, such as "Uncle Howard is sleeping, took a trip, went away or went to heaven." *(Religious, spiritual or cultural explanations need to follow the use of the word "died".)* Discuss the fact that Uncle Howard is no longer in pain. Respect the young person's fears. Answer **all** questions with honest, matter-of-fact information. "That's a good question" is usually a confirming start to the conversation.

2. In illness and injury, discuss the fact that Beth may be in pain and there may be a greater need to be quiet so Beth's body can rest and heal so she may feel better soon.

3. Perhaps one of the best ways to prepare children for a serious illness in the family or possibly even a death is to use "teachable moments." An example of this is talking about feelings around the illness of a pet, the death of an insect or even a houseplant. Becoming familiar with the concept of death in a less threatening forum may allow a child to be more prepared when a serious illness strikes or a loved one dies.

4. Be aware that imagined guilt for the death is frequently not verbally expressed and often causes significant emotional problems later. **Listen to** ~ and for ~ these concerns. It is helpful to assure the young person he or she was not responsible for the death, that the deceased cherished them and knew how much the child or teenager loved them.

5. Children between the ages of 4 and 9 may view illness and death in very concrete ways, asking "If B*eth* is going to get well, how can she eat with tubes in her nose?" "How much blood can she lose?" or "How does she feel sick?" After a death they may ask, "If U*ncle* H*oward* is going to be buried in the ground, how will he eat?" or "How does it feel to be dead?" These are not silly questions for children, just their way of attempting to understand about the illness or death.

6. Three important questions children often ask after a death: "Will you (*my caretaker*) die too?" "Did I cause the death?" and "Will I die too?" Reassure children on these topics, even if they do not actually verbalize questions to you.

7. Explain to them that some people they do not know will be involved. "So you will likely be seeing new people around the house."

8. Consistency has a comforting effect for everyone, especially young people. Keep as normal a daily routine as possible, including regular sit-down meals. We have found a blessing at meals that mentions B*eth and* U*ncle* H*oward* by name makes it much easier to talk of concerns and things we can do with or for her and to remember him. It's also fun to recall fond memories and tell stories that include them ~ both during meals and at other times.

9. Realize that even small children can be participants in the family mourning process, including the services or in the case of illness, the support process (*they often find later that it was very meaningful*). Children get a sense of connection and acknowledgment when they are allowed to help. If they express interest in being involved, give them some options of what they might do or encourage them to come up with ideas. In the case of illness or injury, talk to them before going to visit about the possibility that they might be able to be helpful to B*eth* and share their love and concern for her. Help them come up with the idea of being unusually quiet, in addition to doing things for B*eth*, and taking food and thoughtful gifts (*especially things the child makes or draws*) to her.

10. After a death, gently explain what will likely happen during the experience, what they will see, where they will be, who else will be involved and that a service is one way to share our love. If they seem interested, give them some examples of what they might do, or ask if they have questions or other ideas on how they might like to participate. Give them some control; they can place a flower, picture, or object in or on the casket **if they wish.** They also need to know they can decide at any point to continue to hold the item for their own comfort. Reading a poem, saying something or lighting a candle in the service are common choices.

11. Ideally each child and adolescent in the family system will have a stable, caring, aware adult available. It is best if the adult is able to be emotionally present, supportive and observant of the young person's need to express feelings, fears and anger both during an illness as well as before and after a death.

12. We have found comforting bedtime rituals, such as a back rub, sharing happy memories, positive stories, soft music, plus a night light, are helpful and soothing.

13. Be consistent and supportive of children and teenagers during the adjustment processes. **Listen** not only with your ears but **with your heart.** They may need to talk or not, cry or not; let them be with their own process. Affirm them in every way possible. Don't be afraid to share yet be cautious about scaring a child with some of your own anxiety and deep feelings. It is also important to remember to preserve the dignity of everyone involved, especially when anger shows up during a grief experience. This may validate their experience, as well as show them that it is normal and healthy to have concerns and to grieve when a death occurs.

14. We have found it important to keep the family unit together as much as possible. It has worked best for us, when necessary, to hire someone with care-taking experience or to have an alert, caring friend to "play and be with the kids" to keep them occupied for several hours on a regular basis. (*Principal caregivers will need frequent breaks from the confines of caring for a seriously ill person and the children.*) This respite person can **listen** if young people need to express themselves or **observe** if they just need to be quiet. We have found that this is a far better solution than taking them away from the family support system. Your local hospice, as well as teachers, are an excellent source of help or referrals. Call them. This is true with a death as well as with illness or an injury.

15. Eliminate the word **"should"** from your thinking about a child's, your own or anyone's adjustment process. There are often many changes necessary around an illness, injury or death and each person adapts differently. We each will almost always "do what we **can** do."

16. Speak concretely. Listen metaphorically. Children need simple, honest facts but are often unable to verbalize their needs. Therefore look for themes regarding the changes they are experiencing to come out in their play or in other nonverbal ways.

17. Sitting next to, playing, exploring or just walking along together are often helpful and less difficult talking forums for children. Let them lead you in exploring their experience. Driving somewhere together is also a good setting for "a visit." Adults need to think of it as **"a listen."**

18. A soft, cuddly toy is usually comforting and is a wonderful vehicle for discussion about feelings and also an inspiration for telling stories.

19. Children and adults of all ages can be involved in working on a jigsaw puzzle. They can talk or not while enjoying a safe multi-generational activity where it is not necessary to speak. Picking up pine cones or sticks for "fireplace starters" is a more active "talking or not" activity. It is done in the fresh air and can be energy expending – or not, depending on need.

20. Children, in fact anyone, can make a notebook, and/or a diary or journal. This makes an excellent grief facilitation tool, or in a lighter vein, portions duplicated can make a nice gift for an ill person or other family member.
   - Get the needed notebook activity supplies. It's a nice outing.
   - Have them find their favorite pictures of *Beth* and of other family members and of memorable, fun experiences. Stories can be inspired by photos.
   - Remember to continue using a camera; images on film are precious.
   - Get a spiral notebook for an individual, or if the notebook is to be a communal or family folio, it is usually easier to use a three-ring binder so that pages can be easily added.
   - Use a color copier to duplicate pictures.
   - Paste duplicated pictures inside the notebook. The original is then able to be on display or stored for safekeeping.
     (*We have found it is better not to use valued original photos in a notebook*).
   - Have an "I *Remember* . . ." section and an "I *Feel* . . . " section.
   - Drawing pictures and/or using words work well together.

Find a private place for the notebook. Children and young people need to know this is their private notebook and have control to use or share it as **they** wish. Immediate family members **must** know about **and absolutely respect the privacy of the child's notebook.**

21. Encourage children to draw pictures about *Beth, Uncle Howard* and their own feelings. This can be a gift of expression which they can paste in their special notebook, and/or put it (*or a copy, if the original is given as a gift*) in the family folio. Children's art expressions can make precious gifts to *Beth* or to other family members or be placed in his coffin as a final gift to *Uncle Howard* (*again, you may wish to make a photo copy for the child's notebook or Uncle Howard's Memory Folio*).

22. One big difference between a child's and an adult's way of adjusting to change is how a young person will go in-and-out of feeling states. It is common for a child to have significant fear or enormous sadness one minute, then ask to go out and play the next. Adults often find it hard to accept that these spontaneous changes in behavior are normal and appropriate.

23. A volleyball, basketball or baseball – even bat and gloves – are handy in expending pent-up energy and allowing people of several generations to play and have fun together. Physical exertion is helpful in venting anxiety, pain and trauma – the fun ends up being part of the healing process.

24. Provide props such as clay, Play Dough™ (*or help them make homemade Play Dough – equal parts of flour and salt, moisten with water and a bit of cooking oil; food coloring is a nice touch*), a sandbox and toys for expressive play. Adults may or may not be welcomed as participants in these activities.

25. Changing roles in a family is difficult. Adapting from having a well parent, other primary caregiver or person they are close to become ill, incapacitated or die is a profound change. Adults will be served by identifying which roles and responsibilities are lost. Attempt to find individuals the child enjoys, in an effort to narrow these voids created by the illness, injury or death.

26. Venting feelings, including anger, in appropriate and healthy ways can be a challenge. (*Give clear boundaries and permission, such as what is an acceptable place and safe object, e.g., pounding a pillow, kicking an empty cardboard box in a specific area.*)

27. Expect regression. This may be the young person's way of coping with the major change of having a principal caregiver become ill, injured or be excessively occupied with the needs of an ill family member. This also occurs with a death. Regressive behavior may include bed-wetting, clinging to objects or people, aggression, anger, acting out, re-emergence of old fears, adamantly refusing to talk about the ill or deceased person, withdrawal and depression. If you are concerned about unusual behavior in a young person, call your local hospice for referral to an appropriate professional.

28. It may be helpful to remember children's and teenager's grief is often a delayed reaction. If you are concerned, locate an appropriate professional.

29 Children's grief will be influenced by their cognitive level of understanding death. As they mature, their perception of a death will change. Therefore, do not be alarmed if they begin to re-examine grief many years after the death.

30. Check with your local hospital, library, hospice, funeral director and the Internet for age-appropriate books or other helpful resources for children during an illness or for recommendations of good books and other materials helpful to grieving children.

31. Call your hospice for information on child and family counseling assistance. A combination of individual and family help is frequently advisable before – and certainly if – problems emerge. Play therapy is often recommended.

32. Everyone's, including children's, adjustment time-line is different. Respecting and supporting each other's process are imperative.

Questions To Ask Our Funeral Director

Death rarely touches one's life only once. This is my personal reference list of questions for a funeral director from my notebook. These occurred to me or came up in conversation as I have helped other families and individuals.

The easiest way to use this list may be to check the questions you want answered and hand it to the funeral director. Request answers, comments or clarification for the marked questions. I have inserted cursory answers, which I have received at various times from knowledgeable people. Your funeral director or attorney will give you more explicit answers.

> **Note:** *Death is an emotional time. I suggest that every family request and review a list of funeral home services and the charges, along with page 229 before starting the decision-making process.*

GENERAL INFORMATION

1. ❏ What is the role of a funeral director?
   Coordinating details for the service. Preparing the deceased for viewing, cremation, burial or shipment.

2. ❏ Is a funeral director available 24 hours a day?
   Yes.

3. ❏ What is important in selecting a funeral director?
   Reputation, personality, facilities, proximity, prices.

4. ❏ How soon after a death should one call a funeral director?
   As soon as possible. However, we have found it helpful if the family has a "kitchen table" discussion of preferences using the information (on pages 223-229, items 6-41) before meeting with the funeral director. If costs are an issue, request a schedule of funeral home charges ahead of time to have available at the family meeting.

ARRANGEMENTS

1. ❑ When and who may spend time with the deceased at the funeral home? Are there costs for providing this service?
Usually anyone who wishes, see page 223, item 8. There is usually a charge. See the funeral home schedule of prices.

2. ❑ Who will put the obituary notice in local newspapers?
Immediate family or funeral director.

3. ❑ What information is needed for the obituary?
See list on page 228.

4. ❑ What is the role of the county coroner or medical examiner in a death and who contacts them?
Funeral directors usually contact the coroner or medical examiner to sign the death certificate in unnatural deaths.

5. ❑ What is the role of the Health Department registrar?
Register death certificate, mail copies.

6. ❑ Whom should I contact to initiate insurance claims, Social Security, veteran's death benefits?
The funeral director can help you with contacts, as these may affect costs, services and burial arrangements.

REQUIREMENTS

1. ❑ What is an autopsy?
Inspection of the body of the deceased by a pathologist.

2. ❑ When is an autopsy required?
The coroner may require one to determine cause of the death. States have different requirements, e.g., in cases of gun wound or some types of accidental death.

3. ❑ Does the law require use of a casket and or a vault?
No; however, check cemetery or crematory's requirements.

4. ❑ Is it a law that remains must be embalmed?
No, not usually, except with some death causes and in intrastate or public transport of non-cremated remains.

5. ❑ Why is a certified copy of the death certificate necessary?
For legal notification regarding insurance, stocks and bonds, real property and bank accounts. Also for claiming veteran's, Social Security and other benefits.

LEGAL MATTERS

Note: *Consider getting legal counsel on any matters regarding a death.*

1. ❏ Is a will important?
   Yes.

2. ❏ Will an attorney be needed to handle the estate?
   Usually, but not always.

3. ❏ How is the next of kin or executor determined?
   Check with an attorney.

PRE-NEED ARRANGEMENTS

1. ❏ What is the Anatomical Gift Act?
   Body organs may be donated for transplant. (See pages 222 and 312.)
   The choice to donate body parts for transplant is often a very comforting
   one for survivors. Call (800) 24 DONOR for donor information.

2. ❏ Does the donation of a body or organ parts affect the timing
   of the service?
   Usually not significantly.

3. ❏ May I make service and disposition arrangements before I die?
   Yes.

4. ❏ May I pay for my funeral before I die?
   Yes.

SERVICE ARRANGEMENTS

1. ❏ Please explain the terms:

___ embalming	___ crematorium	___ mausoleum
___ interment	___ inurnment	___ memorial service
___ entombment	___ urn	___ memorial service funeral
___ casket	___ niche	___ graveside service funeral
___ grave liner	___ crypt	___ closed casket funeral
___ committal	___ vault	___ sealed casket funeral

2. ❏ May we have a viewing, casket and funeral services if the body
   is to be cremated following these services?
   Yes, but the body must be embalmed.

3. ❏ May we have a private rather than a public funeral or
   memorial service?
   Yes.

CREMATION

1. ❑ May remains be cremated with or without a casket?
Yes, ask about possible restrictions.

2. ❑ May I accompany the body to the crematorium?
Yes. Increasingly, crematoriums are set up for visitors but some are still very industrial in atmosphere. Your local funeral director may be willing to accommodate this request. If this is your wish, it is worth asking.

3. ❑ What is direct cremation?
No services, viewing or visitation will take place.

4. ❑ May a family scatter cremated remains?
Yes.

5. ❑ Are there restrictions on where remains may be scattered?
Yes. Check with your funeral director.

PREPARING FOR THE BURIAL

1. ❑ May I have a copy of the price list for a funeral and all funeral home charges?
Yes. Federal Law requires this price list always be available upon request.

2. ❑ Is it possible to have lodge or fraternal organization members officiate at a funeral service?
Yes.

3. ❑ What are memorial cards?
Information cards that are traditionally given out at funerals and memorial services.

4. ❑ Who should receive thank-you cards after the service?
Persons who assisted the family and who sent flowers, food or memorial contributions.

5. ❑ How many pallbearers are required for a service?
Usually six, plus any honorary pallbearers.

6. ❑ May something special be placed in a casket with the deceased?
Yes.

What are the restrictions?
Size of the casket.

7. ❑ How long after death should the memorial service be scheduled?
The family decides – usually within two to seven days after obituary notices appear in newspapers.

8. ❑ How does one ship remains to another city for burial?
   Your local funeral director will handle this arrangement.

9. ❑ What do you do if a death occurs while visiting in another city?
   Your own funeral director will handle these arrangements for you.

10. ❑ Are there additional winter death charges such as body storage or winter burial fees?
    These charges should be on the price list in areas where they apply.

AFTER FUNERAL OR MEMORIAL SERVICE

1. ❑ How do I order a gravestone?
   Contact your funeral director or a monument company.

2. ❑ What organizations exist to help with grief after a death?
   Hospice, grief support groups, churches and other organizations are available. Ask funeral director for those in your area (see pages 310-312).

3. ❑ How do I find a private therapist?
   Check phone book under:
   Counselors
   Licensed Clinical Social Workers
   Psychologists
   Psychiatrists

   Call **three** *for a free phone interview. Ask specifically about grief training and the cost for professional services. Select the one with whom you wish to work and make an appointment.*

   Some churches have referral services.

Counseling is frequently much more helpful than one would expect.

Remember: It is **NEVER too late** to ask for help!

Other questions to ask our funeral director…

Preparing a Personalized Memorial Card

Though we had never seen a personalized memorial card, we knew the standardized cards provided by funeral homes were not what we would use.

A personalized card was our alternative and was to be printed on a copy machine. The following pages hold examples of memorial cards from my collection of cards sent by people who have been inspired to use this idea for a family member or friend.

Pictures of people reproduce best on ivory paper. Copy-machine-weight paper folded to card size was used for all but the second and seventh samples which were run on 8½" x 11" card stock. By using the space around the picture, Sample 1 was also used for short thank-you notes. Memorial cards 3 and 6 also served as printed thank-you and acknowledgment cards, as well as being used at the service. All of these cards were included with holiday correspondence (*see pages* 291-294) to inform those who did not already know of the death. Matching 4½" x 5¾" envelopes were used to coordinate the mailing.

Step 1: Select materials to be included, such as:

❏ Picture (*if professional photo*)*   ❏ Artwork or borders
❏ Poem*   ❏ Birth – death dates and places
❏ Map to after-service gathering   ❏ Words to songs*
❏ Memorial organization address   *Remember to acknowledge the source.*

Step 2: Design, lay out, paste up and take camera-ready art to printer or copy center. It may be easiest to call a graphic artist unless you have the necessary equipment and skills. Printers and copy centers often have graphic artists on staff. Designers are usually listed under "Graphics" in the Yellow Pages.

Step 3: Explain to the graphic artist on the phone what you need and the time schedule. Make an appointment. Ask for a written cost estimate for the job. If the card is no more involved than the examples shown in this section, the cost will likely be minimal.

Step 4: Take the following to the appointment:

• Selected materials from **Step 1**
• List of questions: ❏ Design questions
                      ❏ When will the job be completed?
                      ❏ May I have a written estimate of costs?

Step 5: Call the artist at the appointed completion time. Before taking your card to the printer or copy center, check it **very** carefully. Reading it backwards helps discover errors. Have several others proofread it for you.

Step 6: Be sure the printer or copy machine operator gives you a written cost estimate, as well as a delivery time, at least 12 hours prior to time of service.

Sample 1

In loving memory of Derek...

(*Cover*)

(run double sided, on 8½" x 11" paper, folded as note)

Sample 1   (run double sided, on 8½" x 11" paper, folded as note)

A Child Is Loaned

"I'll lend you for a little time a child of mine, He said.
For you to love the while he lives and mourn for when he's dead.
It may be moments, months, thirteen years or fifty-five.
But will you, till I call him back, take care of him for me?
He'll bring his charms to gladden you,
as well as frustrations that will help you grow.

Should his stay be brief,
you'll have his lovely memories as solace for your grief.
I cannot promise he will stay since all from earth return.
There are lessons I want this child to learn.
I've looked this wide world over in my search for teachers true.
From the throngs that crowd life's lanes, I have selected you."

"Now will you give him all your love nor think the labor vain,
when I come to call and take him back again?"

"I think I heard us answer God. 'Dear Lord, Thy will be done.'
For all the joy Thy child shall bring, the risk of grief we'll run.
We'll shelter him with tenderness, we'll love him while we may.
And for all the happiness we've known, forever grateful stay.
Should his flight be called much sooner than we've planned,
we'll brave the bitter grief that comes and try to understand."

Unknown

In Memory of
Derek Andrew Davies

Born
February 5, 1971
Oxnard, California

Died
August 24, 1984
San Luis Obispo, California

Memorial Service
August 29, 1984
11:00 A.M.
United Methodist Church
San Luis Obispo

(*Inside*)

Note: *Two different handwritten versions of this poem were left by visitors to our home the weekend after Derek's death. Both pieces were titled 'A Child Is Loaned' and identified the author as Unknown. On Monday, we chose this version for Derek's memorial card to be used at his service on Wednesday.*
   Later, upon checking, it appears that these pieces were altered versions of an Edgar Guest poem, 'To All Parents.'

Sample 1

Life Is for Living

Life is for living, whatever you will live for
you will give.
Life is for giving, whatever you will give
to life will live.
Life is for doing, for living, giving, doing,
learning how.
Life is for you and life is for me.
Life is for living now!

Life is for loving, whatever you will love
enough is yours.
Life is for sharing, whatever you will share
with others grows.
Life is for being, for loving, sharing,
being, learning how.
Life is for you and life is for me.
Life is for living now!
Life is for living now!

Freely, Freely

God gave me love in Jesus' name
I've been born in Jesus' name
And in Jesus' name I come to you
To share His love
as He told me to.

He said,
"Freely, freely you have received,
Freely, freely give.
Go in my name
and because you believe,
others will know that I live."

All power is given in Jesus' name
In earth and heaven in Jesus' name
And in Jesus' name I come to you
To share His power
as He told me to.

Bind Us Together

Bind us together Lord,
bind us together with cords
that cannot be broken.
Bind us together Lord
bind us together
bind us together with love.

There is only one God
there is only one King
there is only one Body
that is why we sing.

Bind us together…

Let There Be Peace

Let there be Peace on Earth,
And let it begin with me.
Let there be Peace on Earth,
The peace that was meant to be.
With God as our Father (Mother),
Family all are we.
Let us walk with each other,
In perfect Harmony.
Let Peace begin with me,
Let this be the moment now.
With every breath I take,
Let this be my joyful vow –
To take each moment
and live each moment
in peace eternally.
Let there be Peace on Earth,
and let it begin with me.

Gifts in memory of Derek
may be sent to
World Neighbors
4127 NW 122 Street, Oklahoma City, OK 73120

(Opened Out)

Sample 2   (run two cards per page,
double sided on 8½" x 11" card stock, cut in half)

In memory of
Julianne Frey

Chapel Hill Public Library
523 East Franklin Street
Chapel Hill, North Carolina 27514

(*Cover*)

Dear Friends,

As you may know, Julie died on October 4. She was at home with us and the things she loved. We know you share our sadness and our loss. Your love and concern for her and for us are deeply appreciated.

She loved stories. It would be a great source of support for us if you and others who knew her would jot down your memories and thoughts of Julie. Please send them – or anything else you feel might honor her memory – for a collection of memories. A compilation of this will be healing for us and we hope it will be a memorable gift to you.

You also know she loved books and served on the Board of Friends of the Chapel Hill Public Library. Her memorial fund will be used for "a special space" in the new library. It will be a space she would love to enjoy.

Thank you for your help and support during this difficult time. It is not easy to anticipate our lives without Julie. With stories and time with friends in years to come, we will continue to grow in our appreciation of her gifts to all of us.

John   Ben

(*Inside*)

Sample 3

(run on 8½" x 11" paper, folded as note)

Photo Courtesy of Times Press Recorder

(Cover)

Joe Vieira
1916 - 1986

On May 17, 1986, Daddy passed away quietly at home in his sleep. No pain, no illness, just everlasting peace. He never feared death because he was so happy with life.

Simple things gave him pleasure. Small talk in the morning over coffee with "The Boys." A drive up the coast with friends. Watching the vegetables grow in the garden, or the honeysuckle creep up the vines.

He always enjoyed a party. Everyone was welcome at his table, either for dinner or a friendly game of cards; he wasn't particular. His clever sense of humor made everyone feel at home.

He loved a good parade, waving at his friends from atop his horse. He was most at home on horseback. A neighbor's roundup or friendly ride, it didn't matter. Retirement for Daddy was an excuse to ride his horses.

His sudden passing has left a great void in our lives. We will miss him deeply. But for all the pain we feel, it is made bearable because of our dear friends.

We can never express our gratitude to all of you. The friendship and caring, special acts of kindness and words of comfort. The many gifts of flowers and food, cards and Masses. Each embrace, every prayer have made us that much stronger and so very proud to be his family. We are very lucky to have had such a man for a husband, father and friend. When it was time to say good-bye, we had all of you to help.

Mary, Mechell, Dale, Mark, Mike, Martha, Mitch, Rosalind

(Inside)

Sample 4

(run on 8½" x 11" paper, folded as note)

(*Cover*)

In memory of

Adrian Carpenter Weir

It was hard to get them to understand me
and
I was here only a short time.

I taught them tolerance and understanding
and
I will be with them always…

I may not have known how to walk
but
I have helped to guide my family's lives.

Adrian

Services
Reis Chapel
991 Nipomo St.
San Luis Obispo, California

1:00 P.M.

by
Rev. Deane Keller
of
Grace Church

Born
October 5, 1986
San Luis Obispo

Died
December 2, 1989
Los Angeles

(*Inside*)

Sample 5

(run on 8½" x 11" paper, folded as note)

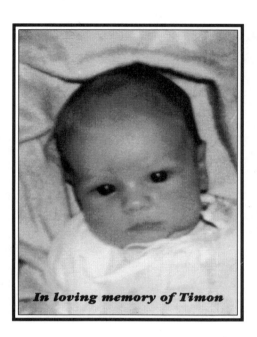

In loving memory of Timon

Donations in memory of
Timon
will be used for research
SIDS Foundation of Southern California
P.O. Box 90544
Pasadena, California 91109

(Cover)

TIMON

Beautiful Baby
Soul so pure
Mine to keep
I was sure

Big dark eyes
Deep and free
Was there a message
I did not see

Beautiful Baby
Safe and warm
Tucked in your bed
Away from harm

Sweet little boy
Asleep one night
Joined the Angels
In their flight

Beautiful Baby
Your stay so brief
Left those who loved you
Infinite grief
        Susie (McCarthy) Schmidt

Timon Alan McCarthy

Born
June 19, 1972

Coquille, Oregon

Died of SIDS
(Sudden Infant Death Syndrome)

July 13, 1972

Bandon, Oregon

Note: *This poem was written and the card was designed twenty-four years after Timon's death. It was a loving and healing remembrance project for his family.*

Sample 6

(run on 8½" x 11" paper, folded as note)

hen I leave you don't weep for me.
Pass the wine around and remember
How my laughing pleased you.
Look at one another, smiling,
And don't forget about touching.
Sing the songs that I loved best
And dance one time all together.
As for me, I'll be off, running
Somewhere on the beach, and I'll fly
To the top of the tree I always meant to climb,
When you're ready, I'll be there —
Waiting for you
Take your time. *In Loving Memory*

DELIA ERVING REINERT

Arrangements by
CHAPEL OF THE ROSES

WILKINS – Atascadero
P R I N T E R S

(Cover)

DELIA ERVING REINERT

Born
March 15, 1912
Monrovia, California

Entered Into Rest
March 7, 1992
Paso Robles, California

Memorial Services from
CHAPEL OF THE ROSES

Officiating
Rev. Les Allen
Rev. Jim Damewood

(Inside)

Sample 7

(run one card per page,
double-sided on 8½" x 11" card stock)

(Cover)

All the lives going along together every life is a full life and is completed every moment it is completed

i carry your heart with me
        (i carry it in my heart)
i am never without it
        (anywhere i go you go,
my dear; and whatever is done
by only me is your doing, my darling)
                        i fear

no fate (for you are my fate, my sweet) i want
no world (for beautiful you are my world, my true)
and it's you are whatever a moon has always meant
and whatever a sun will always sing is you

here is the deepest secret nobody knows
(here is the root of the root and the bud of the bud
and the sky of the sky of a tree called life; which grows
higher than soul can hope or mind can hide)
and this is the wonder that's keeping the stars apart

i carry your heart (i carry it in my heart)

                        e.e. cummings

In memory of
Brett Damon Gillespie

Born
November 3, 1970

Died
January 29, 1986

Memorial Service
February 3, 1986
3:30 P.M.

United Methodist Church
San Luis Obispo

or finished or over every moment it begins all over again. We are.

We live. We love. Across a void of mystery and dread bid the tender light of faith to share.

(Inside)

Insert Ideas

(run on 8½" x 11" paper, four notes to the page, cut and inserted into the memorial card)

It may be helpful in saying good-bye to Derek to share how,

I Remember Derek ...

_____

_____

_____

_____

_____

_____

_____

_____

_____

_____

_____

_____

(Please consider including what happened, when, where, how you felt, what you learned.)

(over)

Dear Family and Friends,
    We would like to take this opportunity to thank you for your caring and thoughtful support in our time of need. Through phone calls, cards, letters, flowers, food and donations, we felt the strength and support from the people who held our mother in the highest regard. As the front of this card says, "...remember how my laughing pleased you," we would like you to remember her joyful spirit is with us. Thank you again for your kind thoughtfulness. It was very much appreciated.

    Sincerely,

    Marilyn Perry
    Diana Miller
    Karen Goodwin

_____

_____

_____

_____

_____

(back side of *I Remember...* card)

_____

_____

Your Name
Address
Phone   *(incase the family would like to call you)*

Thank you for sharing your memory.
This card will be placed with pictures of him in the
Memorial Book for Derek.

Please place in basket near the guest book as you leave this memorial service or mail it as soon as possible to:
    1345 Broad Street, San Luis Obispo, CA 93401

(duplicate note)

Ideas for memorial cards...

Memorial or Funeral Service Details, Other Types of Services and Grief-Related Experiences

The purpose of a memorial service is to help people say good-bye to a loved one in a positive way. There are important decisions in preparing for a memorial service. Tradition need not bind the experience.

Increasingly, memorial and funeral services are participatory celebrations, facilitated by a family member, friend or clergy. When shared in this way, memories of a person's life are a beautiful gift to everyone present. Videotaping technology makes it possible to give this opportunity to future generations and those not able to come. Parameters of traditional services seem to be widening (*see notes on pages 235 and 273 plus 178-200 for actual service example*).

BEFORE PLANNING THE SERVICE

Call the attorney holding a copy of the will. The immediate family will need to locate the burial and upon-death instructions and provide the name of the executor. If there are no will, no instructions and no executor named, the family will have to make many more decisions. In most cases, it is possible to choose whether or not — and to what degree — you wish assistance from clergy.

DATE OF SERVICE

1. Usually the service is held within two to seven days after the death and at least two days after obituary notices appear in newspapers. Friday or weekend services are helpful for those who travel a distance. Long delays between a death and the service are often hard emotionally for survivors.
2. Allow travel time for those coming some distance.

HOUR OF SERVICE

1. An 11:00 a.m. service may allow working people to participate more easily.
➼ 2. Time of service should be set after school if many young people are likely to be involved.
3. A convenient time for a meal-centered gathering afterwards. (*Sharing food encourages a leisurely and relaxed atmosphere for family and friends who may not know each other.*)

➼ Children or Youth

PLACE OF SERVICE

1. If held at a church, choose one of appropriate size and denomination.
2. If outside a church, choose a location that is easy to find.

MEMORIAL CARDS

1. Regular, funeral home style
2. Personalized (*see page 256 and samples on pages 257-266*)
   Consider including:
   ❑ picture of the deceased*
   ❑ poem*
   ❑ birth and death dates and places
   ❑ words to be sung and/or repeated at service*
   ❑ address of Memorial Fund (*Donors usually appreciate the privacy of donating to an institution rather than to a family memorial address.*)
   ❑ map or address of after-service gathering location
     * *Remember to include credit lines for sources*

FLOWERS (*specific types of flowers and objects can be worked into arrangements*)

1. Altar flowers
2. A regular casket spray.
3. A casket spray of flowers or greens with a few flowers (As *attendees exit past the closed casket, they can each add a flower from a convenient container. This allows those present thoughtful and easily accomplished participation in the service.*)
4. Memorial donations are often suggested in lieu of additional flowers.

MUSIC AT SERVICE

1. Instrumental or vocal — taped or live.
2. Select musicians or ask for recommendations from clergy or funeral director.
3. Specify what songs the family wishes to use. It is helpful for you to give musicians preference guidelines regarding the type of music if songs are not specified.

Note: *Be sure to mention songs or types of music that would be unacceptable to family members.* **Listen** *to* **both words** *and the* **music before** *making final selections.*

PARTICIPANTS AT SERVICE (*any or all of these*)

1. Family
2. Clergy (*usually appreciate family participation*)
3. Friends, business associates and professionals
4. Audience (*Service facilitator needs to carry a microphone into the audience.*)

ORDER OF SERVICE   (*Common length for a service is 45 minutes to one hour – range is usually 25 minutes to two hours.*)

Music	• played as people arrive and exit
Opening	• states the reason for gathering, usually along with prayer, Scripture reading, poem or other material
Singing	• may be solo, choral or attendees
Service	• liturgy, remembrances by family and friends (*telling of experiences — humorous, good and hard times*)
Announcement	• invitation to after-service gathering, including location — or posted maps at door
Closing	• possibly combines songs, Scripture reading, poetry or prayer

INTERMENT

1. Public or private
2. By clergy
3. Only by family

MISCELLANEOUS ITEMS

1. Record the service on videotape. (*This is a valuable grief tool for those unable to attend. Later, it is a wonderful way to share a person's life and accomplishments with children and adults who came into the family after the person died.*)

2. After-service gatherings are very important. They allow friends and family to be together in a relaxed atmosphere. (*For us, this launched our healing of grief.*) See page 236.

   Remember: *Friends want to help in any way they can. A potluck-style gathering is usually the easiest and provides a way for friends to assist. This also provides the grieving family with food for several days.*

3. Preferences of the deceased and of family members are important guides in planning services.

4. Books the deceased used and loved are often marked or contain clippings, underlining and other usable memorial service material.

5. Nurses, other professionals and caregivers frequently appreciate the offer to be involved or included in the service, since a close relationship often evolves in cases of prolonged illness.

6. A memorial record book and/or a homemade folio notebook (*see pages* 219, 239, 242 *and* 260) which includes a guest register is meaningful for most families.

7. A display of meaningful objects and pictures is worth the effort. Placing convenient memorial organization donation envelopes discretely at the edge of the display is often appreciated by attendees.

➠8. Don't exclude the children from — or force them to participate in — the family mourning process, including the services. Explain ahead of time what will happen, what they will see, where they will be and that a service is one way to share our love. **Then** ask them how they might like to participate (*see pages 246-249 on Children and Death*).

➠9. Even small children can participate in services (*if they want to be included*). Give them some control. They can place a flower, picture, drawing or object of their creation in or on the casket, if they wish, or they can continue to hold the item for their own comfort.

10. I *Remember* ... cards can be designed to be given out to attendees at the memorial or funeral service. The cards can be returned to a basket as people exit the service or be returned by mail to an address printed on the back of the card. They are then placed with photographs of the deceased in a memorial album or folio notebook for the family. The card can be designed to encourage people to include what happened, when, where, how, what was felt, what was learned. Include a place to sign and date the small card (*see page 265 for an example*).

11. As part of an outdoor service, flowers or leaves (*representing memories*) can be gently placed in a creek or on the ocean (*with the tide going out*). An alternative (*non-location bound*) is a Circle of Memories gathering around the grave, casket or urn. Each participant relates a memory, reads a poem or paragraph.

Other Types of Services and Grief-Related Experiences

There are many other events that can be exquisite memorial experiences. Following are a few we have used or in which we have been participants. Creativity in meeting the needs of those involved is what is important.

A LIVING SERVICE
"This Is Your Life" or *"Thank You for Being Part of My Life"*

Recently, I have been told of very meaningful pre-death "This Is Your Life" or "Thank You for Being Part of My Life" services. These are held with the very ill person present and with their involvement in the planning. These are usually in a hospital chapel, in a hospital garden, or other meaning-filled and convenient setting, with the dying person present. Clergy may or may not participate. All of the elements of a memorial service can be included for a logical flow to the experience (*see Order of Service, page* 271).

The important people in the person's life, family and co-workers participate. After a brief life recap, there is a colorful sharing of memories, appreciations, laughter and love. "It is an unforgettable and beautiful 'Thank You' for life, love, accomplishment and friendship."

This service can be held in addition to an after-death service.

A HOSPICE HOLIDAY SERVICE
"They Touched Our Life"

Each year during the holidays many hospices hold a service and remembrance reception for the families of all clients who have died during the year. A common way of doing this service is to ask each family to provide a favorite picture of the deceased. The pictures are converted to slides, and while soothing music is played, the slides are slowly shown.

This is a lovely support gesture and an acknowledgment of the fact that holidays are difficult after a loss. It also gives people an opportunity to meet others who have had a similar experience and loss during the last year. This is a point of possibly increased comfort for those who resist support groups. Involvement in a support group may be a result for attendees.

INFANT, STILLBIRTH AND MISCARRIAGE
HOSPITAL MEMORIAL SERVICE

Twenty-four years after our son Dylan's death, while on a book tour, I participated in a Memorial Service at Tampa General Hospital in Tampa, Florida. In talking with their staff, I happened to mention we had not had a service for our baby son. As a result, Dylan was included in their service for the families of all infant, stillbirth and miscarriage deaths that had occurred in that hospital in the preceding six months. At this hospital, the nurses, chaplain and social support staff work together on a service for families who have experienced the loss of a child. Invitations to the service are sent to each family, informing them of the time and date of the service.

Held on a Sunday afternoon, it was a lovely simple participatory service, with music, candles and flowers using the Order of Service mentioned (*on page* 271). Anyone who wanted to was invited to share. Each child's name was mentioned and a candle lit in the baby's memory, whether the family was present or not. At the close of the service, we moved outside to watch dancers perform in a lovely rose garden. A rose was picked for each child and given to the family or mother. As a closing, we playfully blew soap bubbles as we moved toward a simple reception where a table of resource literature and each child's candle was available for their family to take home.

FAMILY REUNION SERVICE OR "HOMECOMING SERVICE"

A death sometimes occurs at a time when getting family members together is virtually impossible. In this situation a service held in conjunction with a family gathering such as a reunion is a nice solution. This is easily done with a Memorial Service or when cremation has been the disposition of choice. The cremains container can be easily transported by a family member to the event and then passed between participants during the service. The container can then be placed or the ashes scattered as part of the memorial experience. We held a Reunion Memorial Service for Uncle Bub who died in Alaska. He had requested to "go home" to North Carolina in the spring. (*Waiting until a reunion postpones the good-bye, unless it is held in addition to a memorial service or a funeral.*)

GRAVE-SITE CLEANUP WEEKEND

Each third weekend in May, our family gathers in Hot Springs, North Carolina, for two days of camping, singing, storytelling, laughter and fun. While we are together, we clean up the family cemetery plot. We place new markers, and weed and plant flowers. This is a precious way for children to connect with their family roots and get acquainted with cousins. We even hike the Appalachian Trail or raft the French Broad River together when time allows us to plan a few extra days together.

ALTERNATIVE COFFIN IDEAS

Our Coffin-Building Experience

Though not a formal service, our family coffin-building experience is worth noting. It stands among my fond family memories.

When our diminutive aunt died at 91, her funds were limited and her independence was very much intact. Respecting her wishes to pay her own expenses, this is how we solved the problem as a family.

She had lived on the Montana frontier as a pioneer. Handmade things had special value, yet she loved beautiful things. We decided the best compromise was a family-made casket, designed to dimensions so it could be shipped in an airline container to her final resting place.

After checking on the requirements with our funeral director, we went to the lumber yard and fabric store. For $83.72, we purchased the following supplies:

8	6 *foot*	1" x 12"	*clear pine boards*
4	10 *foot*	1" x 2"	*Douglas fir boards*
	10 *yards*		*pink satin type fabric*

We had on hand: a wood stapler and staples, 2 hammers, nails, a saw, 2 sawhorses, enough thin cardboard to make 50' of 2" strips (*to staple to the satin for a smooth outside edge*), her hospital egg-crate foam pad, 2 extra pillows (*one for her head and one to cut in half to pad the coffin ends*).

The night after her memorial service, three generations of our family gathered for a potluck dinner at our home. After dinner, with Strauss waltzes (*ones to which she had loved to dance*) and a fire in the living room fireplace, we pushed the furniture out of the way and the project started. We brought the sawhorses and supplies in from the garage. Together — children and all — we built her casket as we told the wonderful stories of her life.

A vivid memory for all of us is of watching her six-year-old great-niece and five-year-old great-nephew, both inside the coffin, hammering the reinforcing pieces on the sides and bottom under the direction of their father and uncle. They then helped their mother, grandmother and I staple the draped and folded satin over the foam padding and pillowed ends.

It finished as a lovely statement of simple elegance. The next morning, the children, their mother and I delivered the casket in our pickup truck to the funeral home.

Later that day, several of us visited the funeral home to say good-bye to "Auntie Vesta." We took pictures of her two beloved husbands. The children placed the photos along with a rose (*the color of the casket's satin lining and her fingernail polish*) in her casket. They said, "These will go with her on the airplane ride to the cemetery, to be next to Uncle Earle."

Coffin Cover or Funeral Pall

These decorated coffin covers may be available from your church, temple or synagogue at little or no cost. A simple one can be lovingly made by a family member or a friend who sews. The normal dimensions are 84" by 132" rectangle. The Pall entirely covers a simple coffin and in some cases eliminates the need for a casket spray.

A Cedar "Hope Chest" Coffin

My friend Shirley's petite Aunt Mary had always told her family, "Never get rid of my Hope Chest." She used it with a counter-top finish as a coffee table in her living room. In her later years she instructed her family, "When I die, please use the Hope Chest as my coffin." They cuddled her in her favorite quilt in her Hope Chest. Their funeral director helped them comply with Aunt Mary's final wish.

A Coffin Construction Kit

I have been told that pre-cut coffin construction kits are available, but have no address. If you as a reader have any information on these kits, I would appreciate your sending it to me at P. O. Box 945, San Luis Obispo, CA 93406.

Other Ideas I want to remember...

What Can Be Done To Help...

These are ideas to inspire you or help you be more observant.
"Two Long Walks" beginning on *page* 206 will give you more ideas.

You may want to:

❑ Go immediately to show your concern and **listen** with your ears, eyes and heart (*actions speak loudly*).

❑ Consider taking a copy of this book to the family to guide them in the decisions they will need to make.

❑ Always refer to the deceased by name.

❑ Do what you can to be sure those surviving eat regularly and are taking vitamins (*they are likely under significant stress*).

❑ Take toilet paper, stress vitamins and tissues to the house (*all are used much faster than normal*). Quietly leave them with a note: "Just in case you use these as fast as we do when there's a group around."

❑ Take food, in reusable or disposable plates – be sure your name is on the bottom (*however, there is special thoughtfulness in a note taped to the bottom of a plate that needs to be returned to you*: "I will drop by in a few days for a visit. Just save this dish for me."

❑ Go to services and after-service events. (*This is far more important than many people realize.*)

❑ Make a donation to the suggested charity or one of your own preference. (*The charity will send the family an acknowledgment of the gift.*)

❑ Whenever you are with family members, mention a fond experience or recollection you have of the deceased (*use the deceased person's name*). Then invite them, in a gentle way, to share a favorite memory.

❑ Organize a support network for food, "a night out" or visiting to help survivors over the coming months.

❑ Mark the deceased's birthday, wedding and death anniversary dates on your calendar and send a memorial donation or a card in subsequent years to family members.

❑ If you are concerned with what not to say, consider avoiding giving advice on either how the family should grieve or on why such tragedies occur. The family will appreciate knowing about your feelings, not what you **think.**

❑ Write out the story of your favorite memories of the deceased and give it to the family. This is good for you and a precious gift to them.

❑ Give the original of especially good or meaningful photos to the family with a note telling the story of the picture (*write date and names on the back*).

❑ Offer to make an enlarged color photocopy of a special picture for the picture display at the service.

❑ Whenever you send a note or a card, mention a memory (*don't just sign it*).

❑ Stop by anytime with a holiday wreath, an arrangement or just a bunch of home-grown flowers.

❑ Call to say, "I've been thinking about you."
"Do you have a few minutes and feel like talking?"
"Would you help me understand what this is like for you?"
"What do you miss most about (*use the deceased person's name*)?"
"It's time to get the tissues out. I need to talk about...
(*use the deceased person's name*)."
"Is there anything I can do to make it easier for you to help yourself through this difficult time?"

❑ Suggest that tonight **you'd** like to go to a fun movie or bring over a fun video and pizza or offer to bring the main dish, if they'll fix the salad for dinner. If they turn you down, try for tomorrow evening. Be persistent.

❑ Invite survivors to go for a ride or to some event with you, as time passes.

❑ Try asking, "Would you like to take a walk?"
"Would you like to take a bike ride?"
"I'd like to have you come shopping with me."
"Please come with me. I want to see..."

❑ Go to the house often in subsequent months; ask the family members over or out to dinner (*be persistent; turndowns are common*).

❑ Get a spiral notebook and put a color copy of their favorite photo of the deceased inside the cover. At the top of the first page put "I *Remember*..." Partway through the notebook start a page: "I *Feel*..."

❑ Go visit with older family members, immediately, and over the coming weeks and years. Let them tell their favorite stories.

❑ Take them a book on grief that has been meaningful to you. Many people are voracious readers on the subjects of loss and grief during the first few months after a death.

❑ When you are looking through your photographs, watch for any pictures of the deceased and send them to the family with a note. This is especially meaningful in the coming months, or even years later.

You might offer or do . . .

❑ Answer phone and take messages.

❑ Play with or watch the children.

❑ Take a soft, cuddly toy as a gift. "This made me think of you or (*use the deceased person's name*)." Often an adult appreciates something cuddly.

❑ Visit with older family members.

❑ Take family members to the funeral home.

❑ Make calls to family and friends for the bereaved family.

❑ Help with creating the memorial card.

❑ Polish shoes before the funeral. Ask everyone who would like shoes polished to put them on the porch by the back door. Bring your own supplies and do it on the porch.

❑ Arrange for videotaping the service.

❑ Help make a picture board or set up the display of meaningful objects.

❑ Make a list of who visits, brings food or helps and insert it in a loose-leaf binder with extra lined and plain paper. Label it "*Guests and Memories.*" (*I like to place the season's name and year near the bottom of the cover.*)

❑ Attend the guest register.

❑ Be a greeter at the service.

❑ Find someone to housesit during the funeral.

❑ Take food to the after-service gathering.

❑ Set up for the after-service gathering.

❑ Transport flowers from service to gathering.

❑ Help set-up, serve and/or clean up before, during and after the after-service gathering.

❑ Deliver extra flower arrangements to and from the after-service gathering.

❑ Help return dishes.

❑ If the family has a fireplace, offer to take or chop wood, fill the wood box, build a fire.

❑ Children love to gather pine cones for "getting the fireplace going." (*It will keep them productively busy for some time.*)

❑ Do the dishes.

❑ Label all dishes of food received for easy return. Take your own masking tape and permanent marker (*for label readability after washing*).

❑ Go to the store. Vacuum or help with other household chores.

❑ Mow the lawn.

- ❏ Clip the obituary notice or article from the newspaper. Send it to family members.
- ❏ Go over, **listen** and just be available to help with chores or anything that needs to be done.
- ❏ Help with a spring or fall cleaning project.
- ❏ Help with a project or fix something.
- ❏ Help address notes or holiday cards.
- ❏ Help decorate the house "just a bit" for the holidays.

Other things to do or offer to do...

Helping Co-workers (suggestions for everyone)

This is a letter sent by previously bereaved individuals to associates of a newly bereaved faculty and staff member at California Polytechnic State University. It has been included to possibly serve as a model for other businesses or institutions. The [   ] indicates that a name, date or pronoun change will help you personalize this letter.

To our colleagues:

[Jane and Joe _____'s][daughter], [Anne], died on [Wednesday] [date]. What you say to [Joe] in the next days, weeks, and months will make a difference. Because most people aren't quite sure what to say at times like this, we who have also lost our children would like to offer a few suggestions about what you might say and do.

The loss of a child is one of the most devastating events that can happen to a person. It is quite different from other, more expected, deaths such as parents or grandparents. When someone suffers the intense grief of a child's death, you will naturally want to avoid doing or saying "the wrong thing." But please don't let your sensitivity toward doing the wrong thing lead to doing or saying nothing at all!

<u>Seek out your colleague</u>. Avoiding [Joe] will cause more pain to someone already deeply anguished. In the hall, passing the office, at the supermarket: talk to [him]. Don't pretend that nothing has happened. Don't avoid [him]. Be sure to acknowledge both [Joe] and the loss of [his] child, [Anne]. If you don't know what to say, simply say "I'm sorry." The words are not important, but convey a sense that you know and care.

<u>Mention [Anne's] name</u>. In fact, look for reasons to say [her] name – now, a month from now, a year, even ten years from now. [Joe] will want to know that others remember and care that [his] [daughter] [Anne] is no longer alive. [Joe] may want to talk about [his] [daughter]; talking is one of the ways of keeping the memory of [his] child alive. Your silence may convince [Joe] that you do not want [him] to mention [Anne's] name. Your words can be a precious gift in keeping [his] [daughter's] memory alive.

<u>Welcome tears – yours and the family's</u>. Your tears are appropriate and appreciated. They speak your concern with silent and deeply felt eloquence. Many men fear their tears, but the parent seeing tears will receive them as a gift. Also, [Joe] needs to cry sometimes alone, sometimes with others. If your words cause tears, you bring comfort rather than distress. Don't expect this to sound logical; logic is irrelevant at times like this. [Joe] will want to cry at times, and the tears will feel good. Don't deny [him] that gift.

Don't be afraid to intrude. Most of us are hesitant to go where we fear we might not be welcome – home or office. Stop by the house. Be helpful. There may not be much you can say, but there is much you can do. Errands need to be run, food arranged, people contacted, and maybe even the lawn mowed. [Joe and Jane] will not be in a frame of mind to ask your help. Just try to figure out what might need doing, then either do it or talk it over with someone who seems on top of things right then.

Avoid saying "I know how you feel." You don't. You can't. Even those of us who have gone through similar tragedies can't know what this death feels like to another person. It is often helpful to share **briefly** what's happened to you; just don't assume it will apply to your colleague. Your greatest gift is to **listen.**

Don't provide a "silver lining." It won't help to try to "put things in perspective" for your colleague. Yes, it could be worse: more people could have died or dying quickly might be better than dying slowly. But "it-could-have-been-worse" will not be received as a condolence. Nor will pushing your religious views help. Hearing that it's "God's will" seldom comforts. If you are concerned with what not to say, consider avoiding giving advice on either how the family should grieve or on why such tragedies occur. The family will want to know what you feel, not what you **think.**

Be there. Your willingness to listen can be a profound expression of friendship. Encourage [Joe] to talk about details of [his] [daughter] [Anne's] life. It's part of the healing. Don't try to protect your colleague, but be sensitive and simply accept what [he] feels or needs at that point. [He] would probably prefer to tell you what is off limits or uncomfortable than feel denied the chance to talk about what lies so heavily on his heart.

Those who grieve are shaken by powerful feelings. They need to know that those near them still care.

Remember [Jane], [his wife]. [She] has an unusual and difficult burden right now.

Finally, call any of us if you have questions. We want to help,

Appreciatively,

Joyce and Ken Brown (ex. #), Industrial Engineering, or home phone
Mary Kay (ex. #) and John Harrington (ex. #), English or home phone

(See list "What Can Be Done To Help" on pages 277-280.)

Note: A special thank you to Joyce and Ken, Mary Kay and John (as we remember Laura and Maurie) for the help they have given to other bereaved parents.

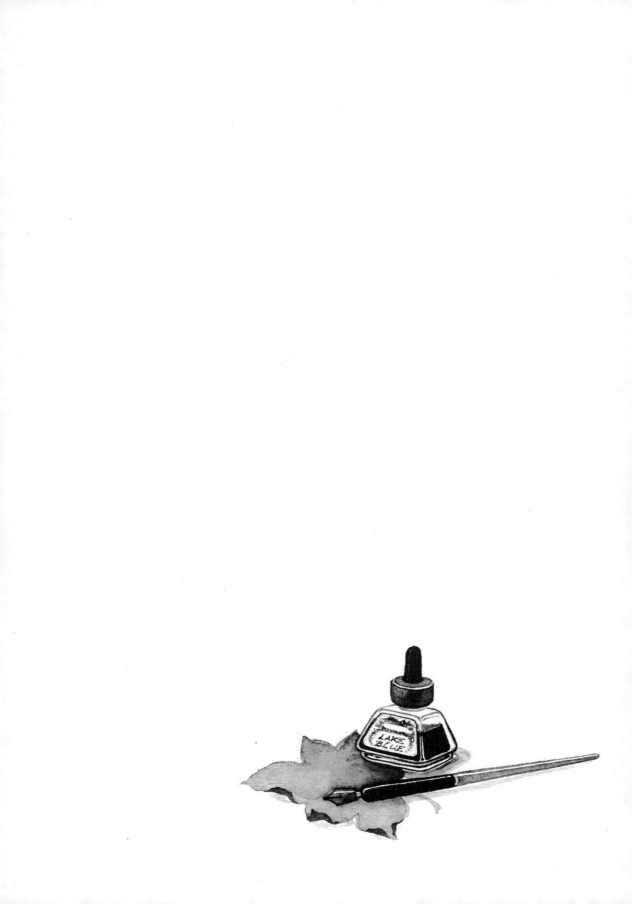

My Holiday Survival Checklist

How can there be "happy holidays" when one has experienced the loss of a loved one? The idealized image of family togetherness over the holiday season is more than unrealistic for a grieving family. The emptiness and dread of the winter holidays make them additionally foreboding.

Lights, glitter and celebration seem to set off our own and others' expectations. Those critical voices in our head seem to be saying, "I should be doing more, more, more." These add confusion, clutter and pressure to the mixed up mass of decisions, memories, guilt and anger inherent with grief. The darkness of shorter days and the inclement weather of this season in the Northern Hemisphere contribute to the problem for many people.

Recognition that the six fall/winter holidays are approaching allows a person or family to move through these special occasions a bit more easily. It is important to anticipate the season with some forethought especially in families that do not have strong cultural traditions. I have found attending a "holiday survival workshop" offered by the local hospice or other groups very helpful in keeping my holiday plans realistic.

- **Halloween**   The death and dark overtones of this celebration make it an important time to anticipate.

- **Thanksgiving**   Recent death makes thankfulness seem irrelevant.

- **Chanukah**   The focus on light increases awareness of the darkness felt in grief.

- **Christmas**   At a time when families are traditionally together, the feeling of loss and loneliness can be overwhelming.

- **Kwanzaa**   This ten-day African-roots-based harvest and year termination family festival uses light and the "unity cup" to acknowledge the death of loved ones during the year.

- **New Year's Day**   Anticipating the year ahead is especially difficult when one is grieving.

The clustering and progressiveness of the winter holidays make them particularly difficult. Most other holidays — **Father's Day, Mother's Day, Valentine's Day** — are perhaps easier to handle because they are scattered throughout the year, unless they fall near the birthday or death anniversary. Remember any holiday or special day may catch you off-guard when you don't make plans to take care of yourself. Memorial Day, the First Day of School (for parents), the deceased or someone else's birthday, anniversary of the death and wedding anniversary are other special days that creep up on someone struggling with grief.

Your life has changed. Accept this fact and begin from a new perspective. Don't try to duplicate the perfect holiday. All of these celebrations can be pleasant and growing experiences. Discuss your plans and feelings about the holiday with other family members. This will help keep clearer boundaries on expectations. Remember that grief is a tough climb and a draining experience. Remind yourself that "I have to stay in low gear to make it. Let's keep things simple." Rather than saying, "I should be…", stop and enjoy a sunset, take a walk, visit with a friend or take a nap.

Consider changing the focus of your holiday celebrations. Adding or deleting traditions or rituals can make an event a less painful experience.

GENERAL POINTS TO REMEMBER:

1. Decide why you are celebrating the holiday. Is it because of your faith or is it for the family?

2. Remember your loved one in name and with a deed. We have found comfort in mentioning our loved ones by name, in correspondence, at mealtimes and sparingly in conversation. This acknowledgment can be done gently and tactfully. Saying the deceased's name out loud helps in moving grievers forward (*especially early*) in their adjustment process.

3. Plan to be with people you enjoy; avoid difficult people and situations.

4. You have new limitations (*emotional, mental and physical*). Choose to do a few things rather than many. Do one at a time. Set and hold your boundaries.

5. Simplify, simplify, simplify. An easy way to simplify the holiday is to ask each person what **one** aspect or tradition makes each holiday special, such as:
   - ❏ creamed onions for Thanksgiving dinner
   - ❏ sending Christmas, Chanukah or Kwanzaa cards
   - ❏ lighting Chanukah, Kwanzaa or Christmas lights
   - ❏ singing traditional songs or carols
   - ❏ squash pie for Christmas or Kwanzaa dinner
   - ❏ chocolate chip cookies for New Year's Day

6. Build your holiday plans to include these "special" requests; keep the rest simple! Spread the word you are spreading out the work! The person who wants cookies can bake them. Help each other. It will likely feel good to do projects together. With people you enjoy.

7. Don't be surprised if you feel angry with the person who died, Holidays often bring up strong feelings of abandonment.

8. Keep the holidays focused on those who are living and what is meaningful to them. Decide which traditions and rituals are most important. Keep those if they are in line with your energy level. If not, there is another year. I like to recall: "If it isn't fun or I can't seem to make it fun, I probably don't need to do it."

9. Plan to give everyone in the family lots of space with blocks of time where nothing is planned. Tensions flare emotions. Strange as it may seem, limited time with the family may be a good idea.

10. Choose to do activities or attend events that bring peace and joy, not pain and chaos. Sit where you can escape gracefully and easily, in case you suddenly feel a need to leave.

11. Consider incorporating some simple, new or abandoned traditions from the religious or cultural roots from which your holidays evolved. This can be done even if you are the only participant.

12. Remember that holidays are really found in your heart. Joy often comes in reaching out to touch others' lives. Watch for those tiny, happy memories in your thoughts and let them lead you in what you need to do. Try looking to find and cherish the happy moments of each day.

13. Accepting who and where you are is the most loving holiday gift you can give yourself and others.

14. Other ideas to consider:
   - ❏ Writing a letter or note of appreciation to living loved ones can be a precious gift (possibly the *only* gift, if your energy is very low).
   - ❏ Write out your feelings about the holidays.
       What may be the most difficult part of the season for me?
       Who are the people who are supportive and "can hear" my grief?
       Who and what situations do I need to choose to avoid?
       What may likely "push my grief buttons"?
   - ❏ Write a holiday letter to the person you miss so much.
   - ❏ Provide quiet sharing time for immediate family.
   - ❏ Have a memory candle burning during meals over the holiday.
   - ❏ Make a memorial contribution to your favorite charity:
       - WORLD NEIGHBORS
       - COMPASSIONATE FRIENDS
       - HOSPICE

❑ Menorah, Kwanzaa or Christmas candle lighting can be a special time for remembrance of a loved one.

❑ Make decorations using the name of your loved one as remembrance gifts to others for their own tree. Save one and hang it on your tree.

❑ A loved keepsake of the deceased can be a precious gift.

❑ Buy or make a holiday ornament in memory of your loved one.

❑ Buy or make a gift or toy for someone needy, in a loved one's memory.

❑ Buy or make a gift or toy for yourself that you can imagine your loved one giving you.

❑ Buying or making a gift from you and the deceased can be also a touching gesture for others.

❑ Make a memorial star or form a star in lights on your house to begin lighting the way into the New Year. (We *put a ten-foot one on our windmill.*)

❑ Donate a book to the public or school library, one you can imagine your loved one enjoying or one that will help others who are grieving.

MY FLEXIBILITY CHECKLIST HELPS IN MAKING DECISIONS
What and what not to do, who does what and when:

Above all else choose to take care of yourself.

❑ Eat foods that are wholesome, avoid sweets

❑ Read something for fun

❑ If you are a person of faith, incorporate some aspect at a new level — prayer, scripture reading, attending special services

❑ Take a nap

❑ Do something thoughtful for someone else who is struggling with grief

❑ Get out of doors in daylight hours. Take lots of walks.

Halloween

❑ give treats — enjoy children calling

❑ go out to dinner and a double-feature movie

❑ bed at dusk with a book in the back bedroom

A holiday trip (*to a sunny or fun place*)

❑ with your family ❑ with a friend ❑ alone

❑ go on a dream vacation ❑ visit someone you seldom see

❑ consider a spiritual or educational retreat

❑ get out in nature; it can generate feelings of renewal

"Going out" on holiday — "going out" on New Year's Day

❑ attending traditional religious services ❑ parties

❑ attending special activities for children ❑ dancing

Holiday dinners
- ❑ have a potluck with family and/or friends at your or someone else's home
- ❑ attend a potluck somewhere else
  - church
  - Compassionate Friends
  - other support group
- ❑ have a small, simple dinner at home
- ❑ have a dessert potluck
- ❑ go to a restaurant
- ❑ prepare special traditional foods
- ❑ volunteer to help with holiday dinner
  - at church • at "people's kitchen"

Cards
- ❑ send no holiday cards ❑ send a holiday letter ❑ send a few

It may be hard to sign individual names. An acceptable alternative is a letter explaining what happened (*see pages* 291-295 *for sample of first holiday note and letter*). Discuss and agree upon possible signings.
- The _____ s • the names of the living •The _____ s family

Note: *We found it easiest to send a duplicated letter or note explaining the death. Include a memorial card in the envelope. Sending them early allows people to respond appropriately without embarrassment of not being aware of the death. It creates less stress for us to prepare letters or notes and address envelopes early in November. Send them Thanksgiving weekend.*

Shopping (*make list of people and possible gifts as you think about shopping; this relieves stress*)
- ❑ buy a nice gift for yourself that the deceased might have given you
- ❑ buy no gifts; instead, make donations to a charity (*in the friend's or family member's name*)
- ❑ buy a few gifts
- ❑ buy a gift for everyone in the family
- ❑ buy something that makes you feel good, to wear for the holidays
- ❑ select gifts for special co-workers and teachers
- ❑ make gifts
- ❑ shop by mail or internet
- ❑ do all shopping in one day, keeping it simple

Holiday baking (*not as much as usual but just a bit with a friend may be fun*)
- ❑ cookies ❑ homemade jams, jellies ❑ fruitcake

Decorate the house
- ❑ a little (helpful in lifting everyone's holiday spirit) ❑ a lot
- ❑ outside your home ❑ with someone helping you ❑ selected rooms

A tree
- ❏ buy a living tree
- ❏ buy one at a tree lot
- ❏ cut your own
- ❏ put a little one on your loved one's grave
- ❏ no tree

Note: *We tried no tree or decorating one year and found it much more difficult emotionally than doing even a little to make the house acknowledge the holiday.*

Hang stockings
- ❏ none
- ❏ all of the stockings
- ❏ all but one
- ❏ put small gifts for visitors in a special stocking
- ❏ Each person who wishes to can write a note or a favorite holiday memory on a piece of paper and place it in the deceased's stocking — they can all be read at a designated time, possibly after gifts in other stockings have been explored.

Do something for others
- ❏ Give a memorial gift to (WORLD NEIGHBORS) in your loved one's name.
- ❏ Give an appreciation gift to (HOSPICE) in the name of the recipient.
- ❏ Give a HOSPICE Tree Light in memory of a deceased friend.
- ❏ Give a "love gift" in memory of a child to (COMPASSIONATE FRIENDS).

Invite others who might be lonely to share your celebration
- ❏ single persons
- ❏ others who have had a loss and might be alone
- ❏ international students
- ❏ out-of-state students
- ❏ senior citizens

For other ideas, send for a copy of:

Handling the Holidays
by Bruce Conley
Thum Printing ◆ P.O. Box A ◆ Elburn, IL 60119

Sample Holiday Note Card

(run on 8½" x 11" paper, folded as note)

Vesta Hughes

1345 Broad St • San Luis Obispo, California 93406 • (805) 544-9038
♻ printed on recycled paper

(Cover)

This Holiday Season

You were dear to our Auntie Vesta,

We wanted you to know our Christmas this year will be without Vesta's physical presence. I know you will be saddened to hear of her death on November 26th. You likely know that Uncle Howard died two years ago. These last years they have been with my parents and our large extended family here in San Luis Obispo.

We had hoped Auntie Vesta could be with us at our traditional holiday dinner table. She just didn't feel very strong. The next evening, I was reading to her passages she had marked in her Bible. While she rested, her breathing pattern began to shift. My father, her younger brother, joined me as dawn slipped across the sky and light filtered into the flower-filled garden outside her room. Auntie Vesta gently, peacefully left this life as we stroked her arm that cradled a pink long-stemmed rosebud.

Many of our more distant family were still in town after our Thanksgiving activities. We were each able to participate in celebrating her life in a story-filled memorial service. The next evening as we listened to some of her favorite music, most of the family, including the children, constructed her casket of fine pine, lined and padded it with beautiful pink satin. This was a precious experience, so in line with her pioneer background, her love of beauty and appreciation of things handcrafted. At her request she has been buried at Tacoma, Washington, next to her first husband, Uncle Earle.

I have enclosed a copy of her memorial card. We want to thank you for the joy and friendship you gave in her life.

Appreciatively,

Phyllis

(Inside)

Enclosed Memorial Card

(8½" x 11" paper, folded as note)

(Cover)

Sorrow

Death brings a darkness into my life.
Cuts through my heart as a steel-sharp knife.

> *Yet, darkness reveals*
> *The light of the stars*
> *Placed in the Universe–*
> *Unseen by day–*
> *and the fathomless depths*
> *Of the Milky Way.*

Oh, God! Help this darkness
To heal the deep scars.

> *May the darkness of death*
> *Help me see*
> *The Light of Thy love*
> *And to turn my head*
> *To the Heavens above*

Help me to know death's not a curse
But a revelation of Light of Thy great
Universe.

Vesta Marie Hetrick
June 26, 1966

In Memory of

VESTA MARIE HUGHES

Born
January 26, 1903
Arnold, Nebraska

Died
November 26, 1994
San Luis Obispo, California

Memorial Service
Celebration of Her Life
November 28, 1994
San Luis Obispo

(Inside)

(*Opened Out*)   (on 8½" x 11" paper, folded as note)

IN THE GARDEN

I come to the garden alone,
While the dew is still on the roses;
And the voice I hear, falling on my ear,
The Son of God discloses.
And he walks with me,
and He talks with me,
And He tells me I am His own.
And the joy we share as we tarry there,
None other has ever known.

He speaks, and the sound of His voice
Is so sweet the birds hush their singing;
And the melody that He gave to me
Within my heart is ringing.
And He walks with me,
and He talks with me,
And He tells me I am His own.
And the joy we share as we tarry there,
None other has ever known.

LET ME WALK WITH THEE

O Master, let me walk with Thee
In lowly paths of service free;
Tell me Thy secret; help me bear
The strain of toil, the fret of care.

Help me the slow of heart to move
By some clear, winning word of love:
Teach me the wayward feet to stay
And guide them in the homeward way.

Teach me Thy patience; still with Thee
In closer, dearer company,
In work that keeps faith sweet and strong,
In trust that triumphs over wrong;

In hope that sends a shining ray
Far down the future's broadening way;
In peace that only thou can'st give,
With thee, O Master, let me live. Amen.

LIFE IS FOR LIVING

Life is for living,
whatever you will live for you will give
Life is for giving,
whatever you will give to life will live.
Life is for doing,
for living, giving, doing, learning how.
Life is for you, and life is for me.
Life is for living now!

Life is for loving,
whatever you will love enough is yours.
Life is for sharing,
whatever you share with others grows.
Life is for being,
for loving, sharing, being, learning how.
Life is for you, and life is for me.

Life is for living now!
Life is for living now!

LET THERE BE PEACE

Let there be Peace on Earth,
    and let it begin with Me;
Let there be Peace on Earth,
    the peace that was meant to be.
With God as our Father,
    family all are we.
Let us walk with each other,
    in perfect Harmony.

Let peace begin with Me;
    let this be the moment now.
With every breath I take,
    let this be my solemn vow;
To take each moment
    and live each moment
    in peace eternally.
Let there be Peace on Earth,
    and let it begin with Me.

At Vesta's request memorial donations
are preferred to the
Hetrick and Hughes Memorial Fund
World Neighbors ❦ 4127 NW 122nd St. ❦ Oklahoma City, OK 73120
Songs are from Unity and Methodist Hymnals

First Holiday Letter   (run on 8½"x 11" paper, folded as note)

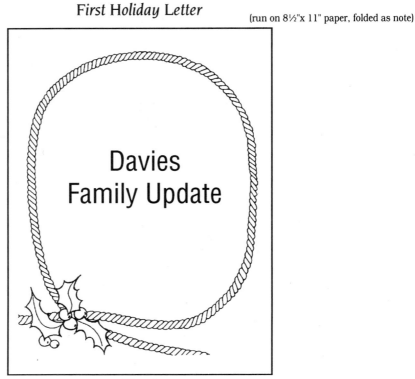

Davies
Family Update

(*Cover*)

This Holiday Season

We began this unforgettable year,

with the four of us enjoying the adventure of
planning what we wanted to accomplish during the
year and during the coming five years. With a goal
of investing in memories, we help the children move
toward independence and developing their own
abilities to contribute to improving our world.

(*Inside*)

(run on 8½"x 11" paper, folded as note)

Dawna was 8th oboist in the California State Honor Band tryouts, singing with choirs, and has been doing some instrumental and vocal solo work in churches. She was excited about being a high school junior and doing well in school yet enjoying, for the most part, her partnership with Derek in the livestock operation here on the farm, even though it meant milking and chores before leaving for school. A university intensive Spanish class at Cal Poly and five weeks in rope with her grandparents on a music tour filled her 15th summer. Dawna was selected as junior class Homecoming Princess, a delightful surprise.

Derek enjoyed the 7th grade in school, 4-H, music and teaching western dancing. One of his goals this year was to learn to team rope. He wrote his own check for a week-long roping class taught by Walt Woodard, the 1981 World Champion Team Roper. Derek's "impossible dream" came true when he won the three steer jackpot at the end of the week, roping against others who had been roping for years, including Walt. Derek's summer highlight was a fun ten days at the County Fair showing one of their Hereford cows and a pig.

In April, all four of us took our long-planned trip to Peru. We traveled with a group, all of whom were interested and supportive of the international agriculture development work done by World Neighbors in third world countries. We traveled to remote mountain villages high in the Andes and out in the vast Peruvian jungle. We were each profoundly impressed with the progress the village people were making in agriculture, health, nutrition, family planning and education. As they learn the simple techniques World Neighbors teaches, these villagers then go on to teach their neighbors the improved methods they have learned and are using.

Parenting active teenagers, continuing the real estate rehab, management and brokerage aspects of the Davies Company, Inc. have kept Bill and Phyllis busy.

Then, as you will notice in the enclosed Memorial Service card, a major shift occurred in our lives with Derek's death in the Wings West airline accident August 24th. We had always envisioned independence for our children but had never dreamed it would come in this way.

Derek waited until Dawna returned from Europe, so she could do chores, before leaving to spend the last few days of summer with his Uncles Patt and Wes at the ranch in Alturas, California, roping and working with them. Four minutes after the plane took off there was a mid-air collision; Derek and everyone in both planes were killed instantly.

We are making adjustments as we grapple with the reality of Derek's death. We all have new awareness of relationships and are seeking the lessons in this experience. Sometimes those lessons are clear, sometimes they are not. However, you need to know we're doing pretty well as we pick up our lives and begin again.

In fact, Phyllis left November 10th, the morning after Dawna was crowned Homecoming Princess, for a trip to Honduras. She is traveling with a World Neighbors' documentary filming team that includes Steve Allen and the Central American Area Director for World Neighbors. Bill, Dawna, Phil and Jean will meet Phyllis as she returns, in Arizona to celebrate Thanksgiving with family and friends.

We wish you a happy holiday season, as we celebrate Christ's birth.

May Christ's peace be with you.

Bill, Phyllis & Dawna

(Opened Out)

Important Information (To give and to get from your family NOW)

Other than drawing a will, I had not thought about additional ways I could help relieve the anxieties of those surviving me until I experienced several major illnesses and deaths in our family and with close friends.

The act of getting and giving clear directions on last wishes frees individuals to live without anxiety about undecided or unclear wishes. I have come to realize that it is very important to not delay giving this information to family members and/or others who will be responsible for following the directives. This is especially true if you have children of any age or are over the age of thirty.

I now have files on most of our family members, with the completed information from this section. Also included in the file is a copy of the Durable Power of Attorney for Health Care along with A Living Will *and/or* A Letter to My Physician, if these are their wishes (*see pages 308-309*), the person's favorite picture of himself or herself (*as an adult*), along with a favorite recent one (*pictures are often needed and are usually time-consuming to find*). I have also asked family members to find a favorite poem and to make a list of their favorite songs that they like and that are appropriate, for the type of service which they feel would be comforting to their survivors.

I am encouraging others to think about their preferences. These choices can be made at any time. Re-evaluate them annually. They are worth discussing. Even as a death approaches, the discussion of these points is frequently a relief to the dying person. If necessary, one designated family member or close friend can slowly gather this information by asking one question on each visit during conversation. Keeping dated, complete notes will be very helpful later.

Pre-arrangement (*of the service and burial details*) is a great relief for most families. The fees may also be paid in advance.

Completing the following Important Information pages can significantly help your loved ones through those first difficult days after you are gone. It will tell them what you want, how you want it and the location of your important papers. This gives them step-by-step instructions and other information that will make many of the early decisions much easier for them to make.

Fill in the following guide completely. If you can't answer some of the questions at first, go back to them later. If some questions don't apply to you, write "N/A" (*Not Applicable*). You can ask a funeral counselor or director for assistance, usually with no charge or obligation.

When you've completed this information, tell your family members where they can find the original and give several relatives a copy. It is also a good idea to leave a copy with your attorney and the funeral home you prefer.

This information and instructions DO NOT CONSTITUTE A WILL.

LETTER OF INSTRUCTION

In an effort to help in closing my affairs, I have compiled this letter of instruction as a guide. This document should not be confused with my will. It cannot provide for the testamentary disposition of property, which can be accomplished only with a will.

SPECIFIC FUNERAL, MEMORIAL AND BURIAL INSTRUCTIONS

1. These are my burial instructions:

   - ❏ Funeral Service
   - ❏ Memorial Service
   - ❏ Cremation
   - ❏ Religious Service
   - ❏ No Service

   - ❏ Interment
   - ❏ Burial
   - ❏ Vault
   - ❏ Fraternal Service
   - ❏ Other Service _____

   - ❏ Endowment Care
   - ❏ Scattering of Ashes
   - ❏ Location _____
   - ❏ Graveside Service

2. I have made arrangements with:

   Name of facility:

   Address: City/State/Zip:

   Phone: (   )

   Contact Person:

3. I have purchased a burial plot at:

   Address: City/State/Zip:

   Phone: (   )

   Contact Person:

4. I would like this person or persons to officiate at the service:
   Name: Phone: ( )

   ❏ Clergy

   ❏ Family member(s)

   ❏ Friend(s)

5. I would like these six people to serve as pallbearers:

Name	Phone ( )	Name	Phone ( )

6. I prefer: ❏ Flowers ❏ Donations to be made to these organizations:
   (Check that address and phone number are current.)

Name	Address	City/State/Zip	Phone ( )

7. I prefer: ❏ Taped music ❏ Live music ❏ Organist/Pianist
   ❏ Soloist ❏ Other

   ❏ List specific songs (by title):

   ❏ Songs of this type:

8. I would like to be dressed in this clothing:

9. Please notify these people and institutions of my death. Make and date a list on additional pages with addresses and phone numbers *(include executor)*.

Name	Address	City/State/Zip	Phone ( )

10. Eulogy materials, poems, stories or meaningful Scripture I like that might be included in a memorial service are or can be found in:

11. Memorial marker preferences and inscription I would like to have used:

ABOUT ME:

This information will be needed for my burial permit and obituary notices:

- Full legal name:

- Nickname:

- Birth date: •Birthplace (*city, state, country*):

- Religion:

- Religious name:

- Occupation and title:

    Employer:

    Type of business:

    Previous employers:

- Previous occupations/businesses:

- I live in (*city*): (*state*):

- I am a citizen of (*country*):
- During my lifetime, I have lived in these places:

- I began living in my current town and state of residence:

- Social Security number:

- I attended these schools/colleges and earned these degrees:

- Honors, scholarships and awards I earned in school include:

- I am a member of these organizations:
  Organization   Leadership Position

- I have held these public, charitable, civic or religious offices:

- I have received these (other than educational) awards or honors:

- I am particularly proud of these accomplishments:

- I served in the military from (*date*):   until (*date*):
  Rank: Branch:

- I received these military honors:

- Veteran's serial number (*if service was before* 1972):

- Hobbies or special interests:

- Other accomplishments:

ABOUT MY FAMILY:

- My spouse's maiden and married names:

- My children:

Name	Address	City/State/Zip	Phone ( )	D.O.B.
_____	_____	_____	_____	_____
_____	_____	_____	_____	_____
_____	_____	_____	_____	_____
_____	_____	_____	_____	_____

- I was married: Date: Location:

- Maiden name:

- Father's name:

- Father's birthplace:

- Mother's maiden and other names:

- Mother's birthplace:

- Brother(s) name(s):

- Sister(s) name(s):

- I was separated/divorced date:

- Former spouse's name:

- Famous family members:

- Family's ethnic origins:

- Facts and dates of historical significance in my family:

Please also include this information in my obituary notices:

IMPORTANT ITEM LOCATION
AND PROFESSIONAL COUNSELOR'S INFORMATION:

Location of item:

_____ Current will (*date*):

_____ Trust documents (*names of trustees*):

_____ Insurance policies (*Do not keep policies in bank safe-deposit box because the box is sealed upon bank's awareness of the death.*)

_____ Auto insurance company & policy number:

_____ Home insurance company & policy number:

_____ Health insurance company & policy number:

_____ Life (*note unrepaid policy loans*):

_____ Other (*veteran's, medical, credit insurance*):

Bank accounts:	Bank Name/Location	Account Numbers
	_____	_____
	_____	_____
	_____	_____

_____ Cancelled checks and bank statements

_____ List of and location of stocks, bonds, other securities

_____ List of and location of other investments

_____ List of and location of deeds and mortgages

_____ Last three years' tax returns

_____ Current financial statements

_____ This year's financial records, bills and receipts

_____ List of and location of credit cards and numbers

_____ List of survivor benefits I am aware of (*veteran's, employee, fraternal*)

_____ List of debts and addresses of contract payments

_____ Employment or partnership agreements

_____ Military discharge papers

_____ Social Security papers

_____ Driver's license

_____ Birth certificate

_____ Marriage license

_____ Citizenship papers

_____ Safe location (Combination/Key [*sealed copy should be in attorney's safe*)]

_____ Safe-deposit box location:

Number: _____ Key Location: _____

_____ House keys and other keys

List of all professionals relied on for counsel (*names, addresses, and phone numbers*):
Attorney:

Accountant:

Physicians:

Insurance agents:

Stockbroker or investment counselor:

Realtor:

Other information:

REQUESTS TO CORONER, FUNERAL DIRECTOR OR OTHERS

In addition, some requests made by you or your family can lessen the grief trauma for survivors. These requests may be made through a hospice or other organization if you are unable to make – or are unsuccessful in making – them personally. **Insist that the request ALWAYS be made in writing, and dated.**

1. The body bag is to be zipped or the sheet is to cover the face of the deceased after being placed in the vehicle rather than done inside the home or in the presence of family members.

2. Family members may request that they be allowed to assist in the preparation of the body at the mortuary and/or possibly accompany the body to the crematorium.

3. An autopsy is either not to be made unless it is mandatory or be made regardless of circumstances.

4. Many individuals and families have found considerable solace in a donation decision. Specify and note on driver's license which body parts, if any, are to be donated for transplant or research and designate to which organization or institution. Hospice and other organizations may be helpful in making arrangements.

   Note: *Accepting institutions usually require that donor arrangements be made* **IN WRITING** *and* **IN ADVANCE** *of a death. This is usually a comforting decision for both the dying person and for survivors. Call (800) 24 DONOR for donor information from United Network for Organ Sharing or for additional information,* (800) 234-6667.

5. Additional requests:

Life-Support Systems Instructions

A Living Will is a document that allows you to instruct your physicians, family and attorney not to use artificial means to extend your life. This is to be done only when there is no expectation of recovery and when such methods will interrupt the natural death process. It permits you to have a choice in the ultimate decision about the continuance of your life. It also should specifically mention the fact that you do not wish cardiopulmonary resuscitation (CPR) and feeding tubes to be used, if that is your wish.

Living Wills are not legal in all states. An attorney, physician, medical association and local Hospice chapters are among those who can explain the laws in the state where you reside. In California, for example, a state law requires completion of a form called *"Durable Power of Attorney for Health Care."* It is important that this document be current (*call an attorney for latest law revision date*). This document, if current, allows the selection of another person who can make health care decisions for you when you are unable to do so yourself. The forms are readily obtainable from stationery stores, physicians or medical associations. Choice in Dying and the Hemlock Society are national organizations dedicated to assisting individuals who wish to express certain intentions. A copy of the LETTER TO MY PHYSICIAN *is on page 309 (if these are your wishes).* Even though it may not be legally binding, MY LIVING WILL expresses your desires, and it serves as a guideline for your family and physicians. **WRITE** your wishes clearly, **DATE** and **SIGN** the document, and discuss the matter with those who will be responsible for making decisions about your health care.

Have MY LIVING WILL witnessed by two persons who are unrelated to you by blood or marriage; these persons should not be your future care-providers and should not be mentioned in your will. It is wise to review MY LIVING WILL at regular intervals; **date and initial** any change or addition. Keep the original and updated copies of this vital document where they can readily be found. Provide updated copies to appropriate persons. An identification card with these instructions should be in your wallet. Attorney-drawn documents are preferable.

**This information and instructions DO NOT constitute
A LEGAL DOCUMENT.**

Sample LIVING WILL

TO ALL WHOM IT MAY CONCERN,

especially

MY FAMILY, MY PHYSICIANS AND MY ATTORNEY:

I realize this is not an official legal document and that it will not
be recognized in all states or nations, yet I, _____,
being of sound mind, do herein express my strong, carefully considered
desires in the event that physical or mental disability should prevent me
from making decisions regarding the prolonging of my life by artificial means.

I recognize that death is part of the continuum of the birth, maturing and
aging process, and so I do not fear it. Therefore, I avidly request that if there
is no expectation whatsoever for my recovery, I be allowed to die naturally
and peacefully and not unduly kept alive by artificial means, including
medication, feeding tubes or cardiopulmonary resuscitation (CPR). I would
hope, however, that any medications that would relieve my suffering might
be given, even though they might shorten the remainder of my life.

Insofar as this document may not legally be enforceable, I urge that those
to whom I entrust my welfare in this matter consider the directions herein set
forth to be morally binding.

Signature _____   Date _____

Witness _____   Date _____

Witness _____   Date _____

Copies of this request have been given to my physicians, close friends and
relatives, whose names, addresses and phone numbers are listed:

Note: *An attorney's assistance is advisable. However, legal forms for most states are
usually available in stationery stores.*

A LETTER TO MY PHYSICIAN

My Death Requests

Dear Dr. _____

    I wish to inform you that I believe in and fully support the concept of physician aid-in-dying for individuals who are terminally ill or injured. If a time comes when I am suffering from an incurable and terminal illness or injury, I choose to end my suffering.

    ❏ ___ I wish to have physician aid-in-dying, promptly and peacefully.

or

    ❏ ___ I wish to have no food or nourishment intake.

and/or

    ❏ ___ I wish to have no liquid intake other than moistening
          my lips or ice chips in my mouth as indicated for my comfort.

(*I have placed my mark in the box and initialed the statement of my intentions and wishes.*)

    I am not suggesting that you do anything that would be considered illegal or unethical while I am in your care. I have fully considered this issue. I believe that I have the right to control the time and manner of my own death.

    I have completed a Living Will and Power of Attorney for Health Care. I will provide you with copies of each document. I realize, however, that withholding or withdrawing medical treatment as authorized by these documents may not shorten the time of my dying as I wish.

    Regardless of whether or not such withholding/withdrawing would affect my time of dying, I want the option of physician aid-in-dying.

_____   _____
     Signature   Date

Note: *Several of our family members have chosen to use this letter. However, because of our religious and ethnic tradition diversity, not all family members agree with these wishes yet we are willing to respect – and have agreed to follow – each individual's signed directive in these matters.*

Questions I want to ask...

Helpful Organizations

Common resource groups listed in phone books in most communities:

Temples	Churches	Synagogues	Mosques
Women's Centers	Hotlines	Hospitals	Senior Centers

Call these national offices for local contacts in your area:

National Hospice Organization　　　　(703) 243-5900, (800) 658-8898
1901 N. Moore Street #901, Arlington, VA 22209
Hospice is a form of care practiced at over 3,000 local branches. Provides a wide range of assistance both prior to and after a death.

Bereaved Parents of USA　　　　　　　　(630) 748-7672
P.O. Box 95, Park Forest, IL 60466

Compassionate Friends　　　　　　　　(630) 990-0010
P.O. Box 3696, Oak Brook, IL 60522
Bereaved Parents of USA and Compassionate Friends are national organizations for - and of - families experiencing the death of a child. They have many local chapters.

Choice In Dying　　　　　　　　(212) 366-5540, (800) 989-WILL
200 Varick Street, New York, NY 10014
Choice In Dying is a national organization that will provide free information and forms for a "Living Will" that are acceptable in the state where you reside. They maintain a counseling and legal referral service.

California Medical Association　　　　　(415) 541-0900
221 Main Street, San Francisco, CA 94105
Medical associations in most states will provide "Living Will" information or direct you to a source. Check for specific documents authorized by individual state laws. California Medical Association has a list of other state medical associations.

HOTLINE (Check your local phone directory) or
CONTACT USA　　　　　　　　　　　　(717) 232-3501
4 North Circle Drive, Harrisburg, PA 17110
Contact USA is a national network of "help lines" - in some areas they are called "hotlines." They provide a free, anonymous listening and referral service to anyone calling them by phone. Check your local phone directory or call the national office for a number that serves your area.

Other support organizations with which I have had contact:

Candlelighters Childhood Cancer Foundation   **(202) 659-5136, (800) 366-2223**
7910 Woodmont Avenue #460, Bethesda, MD 20814

Catholic Women's League, *Tasmania*   **(03) 623-69430**
16 Citerion Street, Hobart, Tasmania 7000

Children's Hospice International   **(703) 684-0330, (800) 2-4-CHILD**
901 North Washington Street #700, Alexandria, VA 22314

Corporate Angel Network, Inc.   **(914) 328-1313**
Building 1, Westchester County Airport, White Plains, NY 10604
(*Free nationwide plane transportation for Cancer patients to/from treatment centers*)

Empty Arms   **(814) 838-6346**
6416 Wyndham Court, Erie, PA 16505

Family Bereavement Counseling Services, *England*   **(905) 770-3290, (800) 310-6301**
16 Arden Close, Ainsdale, Southport, PR8 2RR, England

Grief Center of Wellington, *Canada*   **(519) 836-3921**
45 Speedvale Avenue, East, Guelph 8, Canada, ON N1H 1J2

Hope for Bereaved (*Support groups and services*)   **(315) 475-4673**
4500 Onondaga Boulevard, Syracuse, NY 13219

Hope House, *England*   **(169) 167-1999**
Nante Lane, Oswestry, Shropshire, SY10 9BX, United Kingdom

Hospice Africa, *Uganda*   **Fax (105) 708-0324**
16 Arden Close, Ainsdale, Southport, PR8 2RR, England
P.O. Box 7757, Kampala, Uganda

Interfaith AIDS Network   **Fax (203) 748-2841, (203) 748-4077**
155 Main Street - 202, Danbury, CT 06811

Irish Foundation, *Ireland*   **353-1-676-5599**
9 Fitzwilliam Place, Dublin 2, Ireland

Jewish Family and Child Services, *Canada*   **(416) 638-7800**
4600 Bathurst Street, Willowdale, Canada, ON M2R 3V3

JFS of the Baron de Hirsch Institute, *Canada*   **(514) 342-0000**
5151 Cote, Catherine #320, Montreal, Canada, QE HEW 1M6

National AIDS Clearinghouse   **(301) 762-5111, (800) 458-5231**
P.O. Box 6003, Rockville, MD 20850

Parents of Murdered Children   **(513) 721-5683**
100 East Eighth Street, #B-41, Cincinnati, OH 45202

Pet Friends, Inc.   **(609) 667-1717, (800) 404-PETS**
Pet Loss Support Hotline
Moorestown, NJ 08057

Elaine Winter, LCSW (*Specializing in* Pet *Loss*)   **(801 272-9555**

SANS, Stillbirth and Neonatal Death Support, Western Australia   **02-999 067 004**
Room G9, Agnes Walsh House, Bagot Road,   **03-9882 1590**
Subiaco, 6008, Western Australia   **07-6344 6811**

SIDS, Sudden Infant Death Syndrome Alliance   **(410) 653-8226**
1314 Beadford Avenue, #201, Baltimore, MD 21208   **(800) 221-SIDS**

Suicide Survivors   **(612) 642-7998**
P.O. Box 24507 Minneapolis, MN 55424

TAPS, Tragedy Assistance Program for Survivors, Inc.   **(800) 368-8277**
807 G Street, #250, Anchorage, AK 99501

United Network for Organ Sharing   **(804) 330-8500, (800) 243-6667**
1100 Boulders Parkway, #500, P.O. Box 13770, Richmond, Virginia 23225-8770

Wings of Light   **(602) 516-1115**
16845 North 29th Avenue, Phoenix, AZ 85023
(*For survivors of aircraft accidents, family members of victims and others involved*)

Other organizations...

Helpful Resources

The authors of many books, tapes and videos have gently taken my hand and walked with me along my path of grief. Although grief is an individual experience, you may also find other books, tapes and videos helpful. There is a rapidly increasing number of good resources available.

Your funeral home, community hospital, hospice libraries, local library and the Internet are excellent sources for books on grief and loss and other resource materials, usually at no cost. Explain your loss; the librarian will likely be most helpful.

A comprehensive list of books by specific areas of grief is available in Bibliography on Grief: *Your guide to the right resources to cope with loss and death* by Patricia Zalaznik, Abundant Resources, 15655 40th Avenue-North, Minneapolis, MN 55446.

A list of current videos is available on "Questions of Life and Death" from Film Makers Library, 124 East 40th Street, New York, NY 10016.

The Internet abounds with sites in this subject area. A *word of caution: the Internet presents risks to those who really need direct help and counseling. Users may get inappropriate advice from non-professionals.*)

• Death and Dying is attempting to list every Internet resource on the issues of death, dying and hospice (http://lucky.innet.com/~kathiw/death.html).

• GriefNet, a collection of resources for those who are experiencing loss and grief. It also has a library and several discussion groups focused on loss and grief (http://rivendell.org).

• UseNet and Network Browsers (*both use* Alt.support.grief) are sites for those who wish to receive or give support for grief and other loss-related issues, as are the World Wide Web sites at http://www.dgsys.com/~tgolden/1grief.html and Pen-Parents at fgko8a@prodigy.com) or write to P.O. Box 8738, Reno, NV 89507.

• The site http://www.sunnybank.com has questions and insights on grief.

• There are many grief chat and memorial locations on the Internet both for people and pets. It is interesting to explore and is growing daily. A search of the words "grief", "death", "bereavement" and any specific illness will bring up hundreds of sites on each browser. Explore!!

Acknowledgments

Grateful acknowledgment is made to the following for permission to reprint previously published materials on these pages:

31 *"Untitled Poem"* by Karl Kempton.

180 *"You'll Never Walk Alone"* by Richard Rodgers and Oscar Hammerstein II. ©1945 Williamson Music, Inc. Copyright renewed. Sole selling agent, T.B. Harns Company (c/o The Welk Music Group, Santa Monica, CA 90401). International copyright secured. All rights reserved. Used by permission.

182, 258 *"A Child Is Loaned"* in variation appears to be *"To All Parents"* by Edgar Guest, *"To All Parents"* from *All In A Lifetime* by Edgar Guest ©1938. Reprinted by permission of Contemporary Books.

197, 259 *"Life Is for Living"* ©1967. Words and music by Carmen Moshier. Used by permission.

198, 259 *"Freely, Freely"* ©1972 by Lexicon Music, Inc. ASCAP. All rights reserved. International copyright secured. Used by special permission. Original phrasing, "God forgave my sins in Jesus' name."

199, 259 *"Bind Us Together."* Words and music by Bob Gillman. ©1977 by Thank You Music, U.K. All rights reserved. Used by permission. Administered in the United States by Gaither Music Company.

200, 259 *"Let There Be Peace, Let There Be Peace on Earth."* ©1955 by Jan-Lee Music. Words by Jill Jackson. Used by special personal permission from Jill Jackson.

202 *Telegram-Tribune.* San Luis Obispo, California.

203 *Dunsmuir News.* Dunsmuir, California.

222 Developed with the help of Sutcliff Lawn Memorial Mortuary, Reis Chapels and other local funeral homes.

261 *Times-Press-Recorder*, Grover Beach, California.

266 ©1952 by e. e. cummings. Reprinted from *Complete Poems* 1913-1962 by permission of Harcourt, Brace, Jovanovich, Inc.

298 Initially co-developed by Los Osos Valley Memorial Park and Mortuary, and Pandora Nash-Karner of Pandora and Co., together with Phyllis Davies.

A special thank you to David Kneib and Priscilla Leavitt, Ph.D., members of the National Funeral Directors' Association, for their suggestions and also for the inspiration Kenlyn Blecker, R.N., has given me.

Index ...

Page numbers in italics refer to pieces in poetry format.

I hope you find this book helpful.
If you wish to suggest it to someone
else or obtain other copies, please
write to me at the address below
for autographed and dedicated copies.

I welcome your comments
or suggestions on ways the book
could have been more helpful to you.

Phyllis Davies ◆ P.O. Box 945 ◆ San Luis Obispo, CA 93406
http://www.sunnybank.com

4481